FACILITIES PLANNING AND DESIGN

An introduction for Facility Planners,
Facility Project Managers and Facility Managers

FACILITIES PLANNING AND DESIGN

An introduction for Facility Planners,
Facility Project Managers and Facility Managers

Jonathan Lian

National University of Singapore, Singapore

World Scientific

NEW JERSEY · LONDON · SINGAPORE · BEIJING · SHANGHAI · HONG KONG · TAIPEI · CHENNAI · TOKYO

Published by

World Scientific Publishing Co. Pte. Ltd.
5 Toh Tuck Link, Singapore 596224
USA office: 27 Warren Street, Suite 401-402, Hackensack, NJ 07601
UK office: 57 Shelton Street, Covent Garden, London WC2H 9HE

Library of Congress Cataloging-in-Publication Data
Names: Lian, Jonathan, author.
Title: Facilities planning and design : an introduction for facility planners, facility project
    managers and facility managers / Jonathan Lian, National University of Singapore, Singapore.
Description: New Jersey : World Scientific, [2019] | Includes bibliographical references.
Identifiers: LCCN 2018047478 | ISBN 9789813278813 (hardback : alk. paper)
Subjects: LCSH: Facility management.
Classification: LCC TS177 .L53 2019 | DDC 658.2--dc23
LC record available at https://lccn.loc.gov/2018047478

British Library Cataloguing-in-Publication Data
A catalogue record for this book is available from the British Library.

For any available supplementary material, please visit
https://www.worldscientific.com/worldscibooks/10.1142/11227#t=suppl

Desk Editor: Amanda Yun

Typeset by Stallion Press
Email: enquiries@stallionpress.com

Foreword

For the last 35 years, I have had the good fortune to work for the City of Austin in a variety of executive capacities including Director of Public Works and Transportation, Director of Planning and Development, Assistant City Manager and for the last 18 years as Executive Director of Austin-Bergstrom International Airport. If there is one thing I have learned it is the role of technological and environmental change will continue to accelerate and that sustainable organizations must have effective strategic and facility planning processes in place to succeed.

I first met the author, Associate Professor Jonathan Lian, when we were both trying to expand our knowledge of airport facilities planning at a week-long training session about 14 years ago. Throughout the week, I was very impressed with his insights and creative thoughts, to the point that when I got home I contacted him about coming to Austin, Texas to work for me at Austin-Bergstrom International Airport (ABIA). Jonathan joined us in Austin in 2006. Throughout his stay in Austin, he was a major contributor to the strategic and facilities planning efforts that allowed ABIA to double in size over the next 10 years.

Facilities planning and design is a vital part of successful facility management. A well-planned and designed facility ensures that operations and maintenance can be smoothly carried out for the life of the facility. This book is unique and much needed as it fills this gap in facilities planning and design knowledge. It covers ten areas of facilities planning and design that facility professionals or students studying facility management and project management will find useful. Jonathan is well qualified to write this book with his global experience in large facilities that he integrates with his teaching experience at the National University of Singapore.

The book is practical with examples drawn from various facilities to illustrate the ideas. It is written in an easy to understand manner and will be a useful reference for facility professionals or anyone that would like an introduction to facilities planning and design.

Jim Smith
Executive Director
Austin-Bergstrom International Airport
Aviation Department, City of Austin
Texas, U.S.A.

Preface

This book was created to provide undergraduate students in facilities management, project management and other built environment related programmes with an introduction to facilities planning and design. Its coverage enables it to also double as an introduction to the subject, for budding facility planners, facility project managers, facility managers and other building professionals that would like to learn more about the essentials of facilities planning and design. The ten essentials of facilities planning and design found in this book are distilled from the author's extensive international working experience at large airport projects and facilities.

By learning about the planning and design processes as it relates to facilities, readers will be able to do the following:

1. Align facilities planning and design with the organisation's strategic priorities.
2. Manage design consultants by understanding the planning and design process.
3. Manage the planning and design of spaces at different scales:
   a) room and spaces in a building
   b) building level
   c) campus level (with multiple buildings spread over the campus)
4. Manage the use of existing space effectively in a facility.

This book covers the general aspects of facilities planning and design for students and facility professionals currently working in owner-occupied facilities.

Examples will be drawn from the planning and design of airports and universities which are large organisations with extensive campuses and are asset heavy in terms of buildings. Students that are seeking careers in these complex facilities will benefit from learning about these ten essential areas facilities planning and design covered in this book. Similarly, facility professionals working in these facilities and similarly complex facilities will benefit from a strong knowledge of the ten essential areas of facilities planning and design.

The book is designed so that its chapters may be read either sequentially, or as individual stand-alone references or resources for specific aspects of facility planning, management and design.

Acknowledgements

I am grateful to the community at the NUS Department of Building for enabling me to write this book. The supportive environment was instrumental for the genesis and the timely completion of the book.

Many people contributed in different ways: reading drafts, providing ideas, supporting me through the process. I am grateful to all of you.

I would like to record my special thanks to the following work colleagues (past and present) for their assistance in this book project: Mr Jim Smith for graciously agreeing to write the foreword, Professor Willie Tan for encouraging me to write the book, Associate Professor Lim Pin for his guidance, Associate Professor Daniel Wong, Dr Yeoh Teng Kwong, Mr Eng Poh Tzan, Mr Shane Harbinson, Mr Kane Carpenter, Ms Alison von Stein, Ms Janice White, Ms Chen Min Sze, Mr Jashirudeen A.R., Mr Lee Han Heng, for reading draft chapters.

I am also thankful for the team at World Scientific, particularly Ms Amanda Yun, for their expert assistance in getting this book published. It has made this experience a good one.

This book is dedicated to my family.

Jonathan Lian
BSc (Building)(Hons), MSc (Airport Planning & Management)
Associate Professor
Department of Building
School of Design and Environment
National University of Singapore
1 December 2018

About the Author

Jonathan Lian is an Associate Professor at the Department of Building, School of Design and Environment, National University of Singapore.

He graduated with a Bachelor of Science (Building) 1st Class Honours from the National University of Singapore. He received a Chevening Scholarship from the United Kingdom Foreign and Commonwealth Office to read a Masters of Science (Airport Planning and Management) at Loughborough University where he graduated with Distinction.

Jonathan is currently serving as the Deputy Head overseeing Academic matters at the Department of Building. He teaches facilities management related subjects including facilities planning and design, and fundamentals of facilities management. He is active in the built environment sector, serving on various committees led by the Singapore Building and Construction Authority (BCA) including the Built Environment SkillsFuture Tripartite Taskforce and the Manpower and Industry Development Taskforce of the Facilities Management Implementation Committee.

Prior to his current appointment, he has worked in facility planning and project management roles at large airport facilities in North America and Asia. He is an Accredited Airport Executive (A.A.E.) in the American Association of Airport Executives, and a Project Management Professional (PMP) in the Project Management Institute.

Contents

Foreword		v
Preface		vii
Acknowledgements		ix
About the Author		xi

Part 1   Facilities Planning and Design   **1**

Chapter 1   Ten Essentials of Facilities Planning and Design   3

1.1   Definitions   3

1.2   Recognising the importance of facilities planning and design   4

1.3   What are the ten essentials that facility managers need to know about facilities planning and design?   5

1.4   Essential #1a – Understanding the phases in the life of a facility   10

1.5   Essential #1b – Knowing the parties involved in the development of a building   15

1.6   Summary   17

References   19

Chapter 2   Strategic Planning and the Facility Master Plan   21

2.1   What is strategic planning?   22

2.2   The strategic planning process   25

2.3   Essential #2a – How the organisation's strategic plan drives the need for facilities   27

2.4 Essential #2b – Why the facility master plan
     should be aligned with the organisation's
     strategic plan   33
References   36

Chapter 3   The Owner's Role in Planning and Design   37
3.1 Essential #3a – Responsibilities of the
     OwnerRep during planning and design   38
3.2 The strategic brief   43
3.3 Essential #3b – Managing the selection
     process for design consultants   47
3.4 Evaluation criteria for consultant and
     weightage   49
References   53

Chapter 4   Space Standards and Universal Design   55

4.1 Essential #4a – Space and humans —
     Recognising how occupants and their
     activities impact the size and design of a
     space   56
4.2 People with disabilities   60
4.3 Essential #4b – Universal Design —
     Making spaces accessible to all   61
4.4 Essential #4c – Area definitions and
     measurement methods   64
4.5 Essential #4d – Space standards   66
References   68

Chapter 5   Programming and Site Selection   71
5.1 What is "programming of buildings"?   72
5.2 Essential #5a — Learning the process for
     programming building spaces   76
5.3 Programmatic concepts   80
5.4 Essential #5b – Site selection process   88
5.5 Site evaluation criteria   89
References   92

Part 2 Campus Planning and Design **95**

Chapter 6 Facility Master Planning 97

6.1 Urban planning 98
6.2 The facility master plan – Planning on a
campus level 100
6.3 Essential #6 – Learning about the master
planning process 104
6.4 Case study: Airport master plan 107
6.5 Case study: University master plan 110
References 114

Chapter 7 Environmental Planning 117

7.1 Essential #7a – Understanding the
environmental impacts of development 118
7.2 Essential #7b – Learning the key aspects of
the environmental impact assessment
process 124
7.3 Stakeholders 129
7.4 Case study: Hong Kong International
Airport Three Runway System 130
References 134

Chapter 8 Capital Improvement Planning 137

8.1 Capital improvement planning 138
8.2 Essential #8 – Learning the key aspects
of the capital improvement planning
process and how to put together a capital
improvement plan for a large facility 140
8.3 CIP Process step 1 – Create a list of
potential projects 142
8.4 CIP Process step 2 – Gathering information
for each project 144
8.5 CIP Process step 3 – Prioritise the projects 147
8.6 CIP Process step 4 – Finalising the list
of projects 148

8.7 Case study: Singapore Government Budget   149
References   153

Part 3 Workplace Planning and Design   **155**

Chapter 9   Workplace Planning and Design   157
9.1 Key trends driving change in organisations
and the workplace   158
9.2 Changes in workspaces, meeting spaces,
support spaces and technology   160
9.3 Essential #9 – Considerations in planning
and design of offices   163
9.4 Challenges in implementing new office
concepts   167
9.5 Coworking spaces   169
References   171

Chapter 10   Space Management   173
10.1 Importance of managing space in a facility   174
10.2 Gathering information about the space   176
10.3 Essential #10a – Creating or updating the
space management policy   179
10.4 Essential #10b – Using technology for
space management   182
References   186

Index   187

PART 1
Facilities Planning and Design

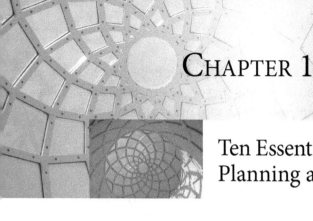

CHAPTER 1

Ten Essentials of Facilities Planning and Design

In this chapter, you will learn about the following:

1. Definitions
2. The importance of facilities planning and design
3. The ten essentials that facility managers need to know about facilities planning and design
4. Essential #1a – Understanding the phases in the life of a facility
5. Essential #1b – Knowing the parties who are involved in the development of a building

---

Essential #1

Understand the phases in the development of a facility and know the parties involved in the development of a building.

1.1 Definitions

We will first consider what is facilities planning and design. To do this, we will examine each of the following words in turn: "facilities", "planning", and "design".

Facilities refers to the spaces in the built environment used by people and their organisations. It can range in size from an office unit in a building to an entire building to a campus with multiple buildings. It also includes infrastructure like airports, seaports, land transport structures and utilities.

Planning and design are the first two phases in the development of facilities. This is followed by the building or construction of the facility. Once the facility is completed, it is handed over to the facility manager who will manage it for the rest of its usable life span.

Planning involves making plans to achieve an objective, in this case, the successful completion of a building. Design is the process of translating the objectives and needs of the client into floor plans and drawings that will enable the construction of the building.

1.2 Recognising the importance of facilities planning and design

The facility manager is responsible for the work environment, the buildings and the campus that an organisation occupies. Having a strong understanding of facilities planning and design is important because this enables the mission of the organisation through the provision of suitable facilities, improves the performance of the organisation and uses financial resources efficiently.

Facilities (in the form of buildings) enable the mission of the organisation. A poorly designed building will neither be able to serve the users of the building well nor serve its intended function effectively. For example, a poorly laid out shopping centre affects the shopping experience and will have greater difficulty attracting shoppers and tenants. Conversely, a shopping centre that is designed with the shopper's experience in mind will have a better chance of attracting shoppers and retaining tenants.

Good facilities planning and design enhances the work environment, and a well-planned and designed building can increase the performance of the people and the organisation(s) that occupy it. A poorly designed building affects the productivity of its occupants. For example, in a factory building, careful thought has to be given to the production process so that the layout and location of equipment facilitates and enables workers to work at their highest productivity. In a hotel or MICE (meetings, incentives, conferencing, exhibitions) venue, an example of this is having a central kitchen layout adjacent to the restaurants and meeting spaces to help centralise operations and reduce the amount of space required by reducing redundant kitchen facilities.

Effective facilities planning and design uses financial resources efficiently. Many buildings have a lifespan of 50–100 years. A poorly planned and designed building will cost more to operate and maintain over its lifespan. This will affect the profitability of the organisation occupying the facility. A flexible floor plan allows for reconfiguration of the building as user needs change and maximises the lifespan of the building.

1.3 What are the ten essentials that facility managers need to know about facilities planning and design?

According to the International Organisation for Standardisation, facility management is the "organisational function which integrates people, place and process within the built environment with the purpose of improving the quality of life of people and the productivity of the core business".

Organisations that own large facilities have an in-house team of facility management staff that oversee the operations and maintenance of the facilities. Larger organisations also have staff that oversee the planning and design of the facilities.

In the past, operations and maintenance staff would not be involved in the planning and design phases of the facility. However, there has been increasing recognition that many challenges faced in operating and maintaining facilities could have been avoided if these staff were involved in the planning and design of their facilities rather than just receiving the facility on completion of the construction process. With the knowledge gained in the operation and maintenance of facilities, these staff can provide good feedback for the planning and design of facilities and pre-empt potential operations and maintenance problems.

An organisation typically does not retain in-house design staff so there is a need to hire design consultants to design new buildings. At a minimum, large owner organisations tend to have in-house staff that can act as the single point of contact as the Owner's Representative (OwnerRep) for the building project. The role and responsibilities of the OwnerRep will be further discussed in Chapter 3. OwnerReps are often in-house staff with experience in facilities planning and design. The number of OwnerReps appointed depends on how much development work the organisation has and whether they prefer to keep this function in-house or outsource it. In some large organisations, the planning and design of facilities are managed by in-house "facility planners" or "facility project managers" that are part of the facilities management department of the organisation.

For the purposes of this book, the term "facility manager" is used to refer to the managers in the owner organisation that oversee one or all of the following functions: operations, maintenance, planning and design.

There are ten essentials that a facility manager needs to know about Facilities Planning and Design. We will introduce them in this chapter and proceed to expand on each point in the remaining chapters of the book. Depending on the size of the organisation and its structure, the various functions described can be done by one person or split up and done by various people.

Essentials #1 to #3

#1. Understand the phases in the development of a facility and know the parties involved in the development of a building.

#2. Recognise that the organisation's strategic plan drives the need for facilities. The facility master plan should be aligned with the strategic plan.

#3. Understand the role and responsibilities of the Owner's Representative (OwnerRep) in planning and design. Learn how to manage the selection process for design consultants.

The first three essentials form the foundation of what an owner needs to know about facilities planning and design.

Essential 1 addresses the "What" and "Who" of the complex process of developing facilities. It introduces the various phases in the development of a building and the parties that are involved. This forms a backdrop for the rest of the essentials. Essential 1 will be covered in Chapter 1.

Essential 2 highlights the pivotal role of the organisation's strategic plan. Facilities must be aligned with the organisation's strategy. For facilities with large campuses, the facility master plan which outlines the phased long-term development must flow from the strategic plan and be aligned strongly so that the facilities fulfil the organisation's vision and mission. Chapter 2 covers the various aspects of the organisation's strategic plan and how this plan translates into the facility master plan.

Essential 3 reminds the reader of the importance of the role which the Owner's Representative plays in planning and design. In every large organisation that develops facilities, there will be a person with the responsibility for representing the Owner's interest during the development of the building. This person will be known as the "Owner's Representative" (OwnerRep) in this book. In organisations that have in-house project management staff, the organisation's project manager will be the OwnerRep. Chapter 3 discusses the responsibilities of the OwnerRep in all phases of the development project with an emphasis on the planning and design phases. It also discusses how the Owner's in-house project team can be organised.

Essential 3 also highlights that the key to a successful development project is selecting the right consultants and companies to work with to deliver the project. In this case, the focus is on selecting the design consultants for the design phase of the development project. This process begins with the writing of the design brief which is included in the tendering documents for the Consultancy Services Tender for the project. In public organisations, the tendering process needs to be conducted in a fair and transparent manner so that the most qualified firm is selected according to an evaluation criteria that is applied to all tenderers.

Essentials #4 to #5

#4. Recognise how occupants and their activities impact the size and design of a space. Learn about universal design, area definitions and space standards.

#5. Learn the process for programming building spaces and how to select a site for development.

Essentials 4 and 5 examine the concept of "space" in the context of facilities planning and design.

Essential 4 focuses the "space" discussion on the occupants or human users of the space and their activities. In Chapter 4, we will look at the space requirements of humans, principles of Universal Design, area definitions and space standards.

Essential 5 applies the knowledge gained about "space" in the processes of programming and site selection. Chapter 5 discusses how user requirements are collected and translated into the size of spaces and arranged into an optimal layout in preparation for the design process. Programming is sometimes either done by in-house staff or outsourced to consultants. In other cases, initial programming is done by in-house staff before it is handed off to the architect who continues to expand and refine the initial programme. The chapter also looks at the process of site selection and site selection criteria.

Essentials #6 to #8

#6. Learn about the process of master planning so that the long-term phased development of a facility campus is optimised.

#7. Understand the environmental impacts of development and learn the key aspects of the environmental impact assessment process.

#8. Learn the key aspects of the capital improvement planning process and how to put together a capital improvement plan for a large facility.

Essentials 6 to 8 cover the various aspects of facility planning for organisations with a large campus. Examples of these are airports and universities which have large pieces of land that need to be developed over a long period of time.

Essential 6 is about master planning which is the key area of facility planning for organisations with large campuses and the facility master plan is the result of the master planning process. Chapter 6 discusses the components of a facility master plan and goes through the key steps of the master planning process.

Essential 7 environmental planning, is carried out for facilities with developments that have a significant environmental impact; for example, large facilities like airports that result in extensive land clearance. Chapter 7 explores how an environmental impact assessment (EIA) is carried out as part of the master planning process to examine development alternatives and how the environmental impacts can be mitigated.

Essential 8 emphasises the importance of having a capital improvement plan to coordinate all the capital projects that a large organisation has. An example of organisations that do capital planning are universities, as there are always new educational buildings that need to be built and older buildings that need to be renovated. Chapter 8 looks at the steps in the capital planning process that seeks to compile all the capital needs and requests of the organisation and prioritise them according to strategic needs of the organisation in order to make best use of limited financial resources.

Essentials #9 to #10

#9. Understand the considerations in the planning and design of workplaces.

#10. Learn the principles of managing space in a large facility with a space management policy and software.

Essentials 9 and 10 examine planning and design issues in the context of workplaces. Using the example of offices, the planning and design for new spaces are considered in tandem with how to manage existing spaces in order to yield the best value for the organisation as a facility manager.

Essential 9 explores the considerations in the planning and design of workplaces. Chapter 9 looks at the key trends driving change in organisations and the workplace. The planning and design of workspaces, meeting spaces, support spaces and technology are considered. It also looks at how to overcome challenges in implementing a new office concept. Finally, it examines the growing popularity of coworking spaces.

Essential 10 highlights the importance of space management and how this can be accomplished with a space management policy and software. Chapter 10 explores the challenges of managing existing space and examines the practical aspects of managing space. Using a case study of a university, the responsibilities of the various parties and the process of space allocation and reporting changes in the use of space is examined. It also looks at the benefits of using software to manage large space inventories and the resources needed for a successful implementation of a space management software solution.

1.4 Essential #1a – Understanding the phases in the life of a facility

The life of a facility can be divided into four phases: plan, design, build, manage. Let us consider the four phases of a building from the perspective of the owner of a facility.

Plan

The inception of the building project could be a problem like overcrowding in the existing facility and a need for additional space. For example, congestion in an airport terminal as a result of growth in passenger numbers beyond the handling capacity of the existing terminal would trigger the need for expanding the terminal or building a new terminal.

The **planning phase** consists of the scoping and feasibility stages.

Scoping of the project must be done in order to outline the extent of the project and what is needed in terms of facilities. This is done by interviewing the key stakeholders and users to establish the first cut of requirements to establish the size of the potential project.

The next step is the feasibility study, where several options are developed, and the most suitable option selected. At the same time, there is a need to secure funding for the project as well as to get the necessary approvals and support from the various levels of the organisation and key stakeholders. The feasibility study is usually done by in-house staff for smaller projects, while consultants would be appointed to undertake the feasibility study for larger projects.

Within the owner organisation, there will be an in-house staff appointed to be the Owner's Representative (OwnerRep) and the single point of contact for the project. He is the organisation's representative for the project to all internal and external parties. The role of project manager for the building project can also be done by this OwnerRep, or by a project management consultant appointed to fulfil the role of project manager.

As a prelude to the design phase, the consultant team has to be formed. Most organisations do not retain an in-house design team and instead hire consultants as the need for a building project arises. The consultant team includes the architect, structural engineer, mechanical engineer, electrical engineer, quantity surveyor and other specialist consultants. In most organisations, particularly government agencies, there will be a tendering process to engage these consultants. This ensures that the procurement of these consultant services is done in a fair and transparent manner.

Once the consultant team has been formed, the building programme which outlines the space and requirements for the building will be drawn up. This building programme is sometimes known as the brief. The process is called programming or briefing depending on the prevailing terminologies used in that culture. The programme describes the spaces and associated areas required for each space. The functional attributes of each space are also described. In the programming process, the user requirements of the owner and the occupants are collected and translated into space requirements.

Design

The **design phase** is often made up of three stages. For the purposes of this book, the stages will be called schematic design, design development and tender documentation. The naming of each stage varies based on the norms in that particular country's built environment sector. After each stage is reviewed and accepted, the owner (client) signs off on the design documents before moving to the next stage.

In the schematic design stage, the building programme is translated into the building's design. There are various schemes which will be finally whittled down to a final design scheme through an iterative process of workshops, meetings and feedback between the owner organisation and the designers.

In the design development stage, the schematic design consisting of the floor plans showing the layout and location of the various spaces and initial design concept is further refined with all the structural systems and building systems (mechanical and electrical) carefully integrated and checked for any clashes. This is accomplished through further workshops, meeting and feedback. This stage is completed when the client signs off on the developed design.

In the tender documentation stage, the specifications, tender drawings and accompanying contract conditions are compiled. This is the final stage of the design phase and further refines the drawings and documents produced in the design development stage. Once the client organisation has signed off on this, a tender is called to select a contractor that will construct the building. This concludes the design phase and the development process moves into the build phase.

Build

The **build phase** is also known as the construction phase. Once the contract is awarded to a main contractor, the building is constructed by the main contractor and sub-contractors according to the design described and expressed in the contract drawings and documents.

During the construction process, the main contractor interacts with the design consultants to clarify any ambiguities and submits shop drawings and material samples for approval by the consultants. The consultant team monitors the project cost, quality and schedule to ensure that the project is delivered within the budget, meets the quality requirements and is completed on time.

If there are any changes to the design, this will be addressed through the variations procedures outlined in the contract and the contractor can claim for additional costs and time.

When the building is completed, testing and commissioning is carried out. A final check for defects is carried out for rectifications to be made. Finally, the building is handed over to the owner for occupation.

Manage

The **manage phase** is the longest phase of a building's life, typically around 50 to 80 years. Regular maintenance is crucial in order to preserve the building fabric and ensure the health and safety of occupants.

Regular upgrades to the buildings are also needed. These include improvements to maintain service standards for building occupants, life safety upgrades in response to stricter fire codes, green building upgrades to improve energy efficiency and reduce environmental impacts and major overhauls of mechanical and electrical equipment like lifts that have reached the end of their service lives. These upgrades could be carried out on an ad-hoc basis or done as part of a major renovation every 10–20 years.

Different ways of naming the phases of a development project

We have covered the four generic phases of a life of a building, with the first three phases covering the development of a building. However, it is important to note that the exact naming is dependent on the type of contract used and the peculiarities of the construction industry in that particular jurisdiction. There are different ways of naming the phases of a development project and the table below lists the various ways. The first three are from architects' associations while the fourth is from a builder's association. Broadly, it can be seen that architects tend to focus on design and break it into three parts, while builders focus on construction.

Table 1.1   Various names for phases in a development project.

	Organisation	Phases of a Development Project
1	Royal Institute of British Architects (RIBA) Plan of Work 2013	Strategic Definition, Preparation and Brief, Concept Design, Developed Design, Technical Design, Construction, Handover and Close Out, In Use
2	American Institute of Architects	Pre-Design, Schematic Design, Design Development, Construction Documents, Bidding/Negotiation, Construction Contract Administration, Post-Construction
3	Singapore Institute of Architects	Schematic Design, Design Development, Tender Documentation, Contract Construction, Final Completion
4	Chartered Institute of Building (CIOB)	Inception, Feasibility, Strategy, Pre-construction, Construction, Services commissioning, Completion and handover, Post Completion Review

1.5 Essential #1b – Knowing the parties involved in the development of a building

The development (planning, design, construction) of a building is a complex undertaking that involves many parties. Knowledge of who the parties are and their role in the development project is vital to the successful management of the project by the OwnerRep. These people could be internal or external to the organisation developing the building.

Internal parties

As mentioned in the earlier part of the chapter, the OwnerRep is the single point of contact for all matters involving the owner organisation that is the client of the project. In large organisations like a university, there is typically a section that manages the development of new projects. The Owner's Representative in such cases will be a member of staff from that section.

He represents the internal parties, which can be divided broadly into four groups: the user group, the support group, the technical group, and the approvals group. Let us explore this in the context of a university development project.

The user group is typically made up of the people who are the occupants of the building. In a university building, the users are the dean, faculty, staff and students. The group is represented by a representative empowered by the Dean of the school to speak on behalf of the users of the building.

The support group consists of staff from the finance, contracts, planning and engineering departments that provide support to the development project.

The technical group consists of staff that provide input on the technical aspects of operating and maintaining the building in the future. This includes the facility management department, Information Technology (IT) department, health and safety department and sustainability department.

Finally, the approvals group are the people that are empowered to give the necessary approvals for the project. Depending on the size and cost of the project, this group can consist of the Chief Executive of the organisation and his team or the Board of Directors.

External parties

External parties include the consultants, the main contractor, government agencies and the public.

Consultants

The key external parties are the consultants designing the building. These include the architect, civil and structural engineer, mechanical engineer, and electrical engineer. In British Commonwealth countries, a consultant quantity surveyor will also be engaged to manage the cost and contracts arising from the project. On some projects, a consultant project manager is also engaged.

It is rare that these consultants are in-house, as most organisations do not have a sufficient pipeline of projects to keep a large number of design staff employed full-time. Hence a tendering process to engage these consultants must be carried out. This is done towards the end of the planning process, which consists of the scoping stage and a feasibility study. The OwnerRep must scope out the project to the level of detail needed in a call to tender, to engage the necessary consultants.

Main contractor

The main contractor is responsible for constructing the building in accordance to the building contract drawings and specifications. He assembles a team of manpower and resources, which includes sub-contractors and suppliers, to do this work at the price and time duration stated in the contract documents.

It is becoming increasing common to have early contractor involvement for projects in order to improve the buildability of the project and get more price certainty in the construction cost. In some cases, the main contractor takes on the role of a construction manager and provides a guaranteed maximum price based on the final design.

Government and Regulatory agencies

Government and Regulatory authorities must be consulted as part of the planning and design process to ensure that the regulations governing the development are complied with. These regulations cover issues such as land use and zoning, fire and life safety, and structural safety. Other examples of regulations are those pertaining to productivity, universal design and the use of prefabrication.

The public and community

Other key parties outside the organisation are stakeholders like the community surrounding the development who will be impacted by the construction and future operations of the building. If it is a large public development, the public also needs to be consulted.

As it can be seen from the long list of both internal and external parties involved in the planning and design process, the Owner's Representative plays a critical role in coordinating the many persons involved in the planning and design of a building.

1.6 Summary

In summary, facility managers need to have a good working knowledge of facilities planning and design in order to ensure that their facility supports the mission of the organisation, improves the organisation's performance and uses financial resources efficiently.

Planning and design are the first two of four phases of the life of a building (Plan, Design, Build and Manage). In order to have a successful project, the Owner's Representative needs to manage multiple internal (user, support, technical, approval groups) and external parties (consultants, contractor, regulatory agencies, public).

The ten essentials that a facility manager needs to know about facilities planning and design are summarised in the following table.

Ten Essentials of Facilities Planning and Design (for Facility Professionals)

Facilities planning and design

1. Understand the phases in the development of a facility and know the parties involved in the development of a building.

2. Recognise that the organisation's strategic plan drives the need for facilities. The facility master plan should be aligned with the strategic plan.

3. Understand the responsibilities of the Owner's representative during planning and design. Learn how to manage the selection process for design consultants.

4. Recognise how occupants and their activities impact the size and design of a space. Learn about universal design, area definitions and space standards.

5. Learn the process for programming building spaces and how to select a site for development.

Campus planning and design

6. Learn about the process of master planning so that the long-term phased development of a facility's campus is optimised.

7. Understand the environmental impacts of development and learn the key aspects of the environmental impact assessment process.

8. Learn the key aspects of the capital improvement planning process and how to put together a capital improvement plan for a large facility.

Workplace planning and design

9. Understand the considerations in the planning and design of workplaces.

10. Learn the principles of managing space in a large facility with a space management policy and software.

References

Ashworth, A. (2012). *Pre-contract studies: Development economics, tendering and estimating*. Blackwell.

Buxton, P. (Ed.). (2015). *Metric handbook: planning and design data*. Routledge.

Chartered Institute of Building (Great Britain). (2014). *Code of practice for project management for construction and development*. John Wiley & Sons.

Demkin, J. A. (2001). *The architect's handbook of professional practice* (Vol. 1). John Wiley & Sons.

International Organisation for Standardisation. (2017). ISO41011:2017 Facility management – vocabulary https://www.iso.org/standard/68167.html (accessed 4 Sep 2018)

Rondeau, E. P., Brown, R. K., & Lapides, P. D. (2012). *Facility management*. John Wiley & Sons.

Roper, K. O., & Payant, R. P. (2014). *The facility management handbook*. AMACOM Div American Mgmt Assn.

Royal Institute of British Architects. (2018). *RIBA Plan of Work 2013*. https://www.ribaplanofwork.com/ (accessed 16 May 2018)

Singapore Institute of Architects. (2002). *Conditions of appointment and architect's services and mode of payment*. Singapore Institute of Architects.

Stanford University Department of Project Management (2010). *The Project Delivery Process*. Stanford University.

CHAPTER 2

Strategic Planning and the Facility Master Plan

In this chapter, you will learn about the following:

1. What is strategic planning?

2. The strategic planning process

3. Essential #2a – How the organisation's strategic plan drives the need for facilities

4. Essential #2b – Why the facility master plan should be aligned with the organisation's strategic plan

---

Essential #2

Recognise that the organisation's strategic plan drives the need for facilities. The facility master plan should be aligned with the organisation's strategic plan.

Facilities must be aligned with the organisation's strategy. In many organisations, this is documented in the organisation's strategic plan. The Facility Manager (FM) needs to have a strong understanding of his organisation and the facilities and how these facilities enable the organisation's vision, mission and strategic objectives.

With this knowledge, the FM is able to oversee planning and design of facilities to ensure that the facilities are aligned with the organisation's strategic plan. In large facilities, particularly those with large campuses (e.g. airports and universities), the phased development of these facilities is guided by the facility master plan.

2.1 What is strategic planning?

Strategic planning is the process of creating a strategic plan that outlines the organisation's long-term goals and provides focus to all the members of the organisation. The strategic plan can be a simple one-page document or an elaborate document going into many pages. A typical strategic plan would have a five-year outlook and will be reviewed annually.

In the context of facilities planning and design, it is important for the FM to understand the strategic plan of the organisation. This enables the organisation's facilities to be developed in full alignment with the long-term corporate goals.

At the most basic level, the strategic plan typically contains the vision, mission and strategic goals of the organisation. The vision of the organisation is what it aspires to become. The mission describes what it does in its quest to reach its vision. The strategic goals are the long-term goals that enable the organisation to achieve its mission and vision.

Since most organisations still use the traditional strategic planning method, this book will elaborate on this process and how the FM may get involved in this process or use the outputs of the process — namely the strategic plan document — to enhance the facility planning and design process. There are numerous books available on strategic management and readers can read more about this strategic planning process in these books.

In terms of strategy, readers can refer to **The Strategy Process** by Mintzberg, Lampel, Quinn and Ghoshal (2003) that outlines ten schools of thought on strategy formation: Design, Planning, Positioning, Cognitive, Entrepreneurial, Learning, Power, Cultural, Environmental, and Configuration.

Mintzberg (1994), in his book **The Rise and Fall of Strategic Planning**, writes about planning, strategy and models of the strategic planning process. He critiques the usefulness of planning and explores the problems related to strategic planning.

Benefits and shortcomings of strategic planning

Strategic planning brings about organisational benefits, operational benefits and stakeholder benefits.

In terms of organisational benefits, having a clearly articulated vision and mission and strategic goals allows everyone to understand what is important to the organisation and pull together in the same direction to achieve the common goals.

Having a strategic plan brings about operational benefits. It is useful for prioritising projects and uses corporate resources in an efficient manner. Resources will be spent on the projects that are deemed most important by the organisation.

There are also benefits to involving the stakeholders in the strategic planning process. This engagement helps to build consensus as different views are heard and positions moderated through the various discussions. Having a diverse range of stakeholders involved will also increase the number of ideas available for consideration.

Despite the benefits that strategic planning can bring to an organisation, there are also shortcomings that need to be mitigated. For example, the strategic goals set might not be the most important, and as a result the organisation will head in the wrong direction. Another issue is the environment in which the organisation operates in. There might be major changes in the operating environment that renders the plan irrelevant.

The strategic plan also needs to be properly communicated to all the staff in the organisation in order that each one might do their part in fulfilling the objectives of the plan. Also, staff might not agree with the strategic goals and the organisation is not completely aligned. Another area of concern is that the performance goals of staff are not aligned to the strategic goals.

What type of organisations find planning useful?

Planning and strategic planning are useful for organisations that: operate in stable environments, are in mature industries, capital intensive, and are large in size.

Planning is useful in stable environments. If there is too much change, planning is not useful as the organisation's plans will not be able to respond quickly to rapidly changing environments. It is useful in mature industries where there is only incremental change.

Planning is useful in situations where it is costly to change decisions. A key example of this is in capital decisions where buildings are relatively permanent and costly to change. Capital intensive organisations are those that have a lot of buildings and infrastructure. These assets are costly and take time to construct. As such, considering all factors and deciding on a single course of action as part of a planning process is useful. Planning is vital to ensuring that the right types of buildings are built and that the facilities are in line with the organisation's strategic plan.

Finally, planning is useful in large organisations as it facilities coordination, control and communications. In large organisations, planning helps to coordinate the actions of staff in multiple units and at various hierarchal levels. The need to work in a coordinated fashion creates the need for a plan. Planning is useful for control. A plan that is developed and cascaded to every unit in the organisation ensures that outcomes and performance may be depended upon, provided the plan is followed and the plan is a good one. Having a plan helps to promote communication, as the document can be circulated to all relevant parties in the organisation for coordinated action.

An example of the usefulness of planning is in airport organisations. There is typically only one commercial service airport in each city and it is typically operated by a governmental entity. This creates a relatively stable operating environment. Furthermore, the industry is heavily regulated internationally. Airports are capital intensive and very expensive to build. This creates a need for master planning to ensure that the capital investment is cost effective. Airport organisations are relatively large, and every unit needs to coordinate their actions in order to effectively process passengers and cargo in a smooth fashion.

What do planners do?

Mintzberg (1994) describes the three roles of planners: finders of strategy, analysts, and catalysts. He also alludes to a possible fourth role of planners where in some cases, planners can also be strategists.

Planners are finders of strategy because they keep track of what the organisation does and find strategies in the midst of doing that. They seek to understand the behaviour of their organisation and look for strategies in all parts of the organisation.

Planners are analysts as they analyse data about the organisation and the environment in which they operate in. They provide the managers with their analyses so that more informed decisions can be made. It is essential that these analyses are made available to the managers quickly. Three types of studies can be carried out. These are studies of the environment, studies of the organisation and studies of the strategies.

Planners are catalysts that promote thinking about the organisation's future. Managers tend to focus on the day to day operations of the organisation, and adapt as they go along. Planners are tasked to think long-term and, in their role, assist managers to integrate future thinking into their mindset.

There is also a possible fourth role that planners might play, and that is the role of the strategists. Planners might be involved with strategy, but they might not be strategic thinkers that come up with strategies because of their disposition to analyse rather than synthesise.

2.2 The strategic planning process

We will now look at the steps in the strategic planning process. The FM is part of the organisation's leadership team and will need to understand the strategic planning process in order to fully participate in this process and help the organisation fully realise the potential of the facilities that the organisation uses.

Once it has been determined that a strategic plan is useful, an organisation will go through a strategic planning process to create a strategic plan. The strategic planning process involves the preparation of the strategic plan, the execution of the plan, and the monitoring of the plan.

Preparation of the strategic plan

The first step in the strategic plan preparation involves creating the mission and vision for the organisation. It deals with the focus and aspirations of the organisation. The mission is what the organisation does and its reason for existence. This is followed by the crafting of the vision which is what the organisation wants to be, a desired future state.

The next step is to do a SWOT analysis to identify strengths, weaknesses, opportunities and threats. This is an internal analysis of the organisation and what its strengths and weaknesses are. There is also a scan of the external environment in which the organisation operates in and the opportunities and threats are identified.

With the analysis of the organisation and the environment, the strategic issues are defined. Gaps between the current state and the future vision are identified. Stakeholder views, competition, industry trends and constraints also need to be considered. Strategic objectives, typically for a five-year period are identified.

The chief executive and his leadership team makes the final decision on the vision, mission and strategic objectives that are in the strategic plan.

Execution and monitoring of the strategic plan

After the strategic plan has been drawn up, a plan for the execution of the plan needs to be drawn up. The strategic goals need to be translated into action plans or initiatives, and who is responsible for the goal or each step, must be identified. The necessary resources need to be allocated, and training for staff need to be carried out. A communication plan also needs to be drawn up to disseminate the information in the strategic plan to all relevant parties.

In order to monitor the progress of the goals in the strategic plan, there needs to be performance measures to track the progress. This takes the form of Key Performance Indicators (KPIs). The people responsible for monitoring and reporting progress need to be identified. A process for enacting changes to the strategic plan needs to be put in place. This allows for adjustments to the parts of the plan that are not working as expected.

Stakeholders in the strategic planning process

Every planning effort requires the participation of stakeholders. The strategic planning effort is no different. A list of internal and external stakeholders needs to be drawn up at the beginning of the strategic planning process. Careful management of the stakeholders ensures that no one is left out, and that the right stakeholders can be brought in at the appropriate time.

Examples of internal stakeholders are the board of directors, management team, division managers and staff. External stakeholders include business partners, customers, government agencies, and the community.

2.3   Essential #2a – How the organisation's strategic plan drives the need for facilities

The facility manager needs to have a thorough understanding of the people (organisation and users), processes (activities) and place (facilities). The FM's expertise in the management of space and its various facets will add value to the organisation. This will manifest itself in various ways.

The existing spaces need to be sufficient and adequate to support the organisation's needs. If it is deficient, the FM will look at ways to enhance or reconfigure the space to support the users. This might lead to renovation or a change in the layout of existing spaces.

Where it has been ascertained that there is a need for additional space, or that the existing spaces cannot be reconfigured or renovated, plans for new spaces or facilities have to be made. This will lead to building projects where a consultant team is needed to design and build these spaces.

Management of existing spaces is critical to the day-to-day operations of an organisation, and the facility manager also plays an important role in this. Performance, quality, sustainability, technology, and efficiency are various areas which impact the management of space and are in the FM's realm of influence.

As the FM, you need to be able to think strategically in order to bring value to your organisation. This requires you to have a strong grasp of the following:

1. Plans – organisational plans
2. Place – the overall area and physical attributes of the organisation's facilities
3. People – the users, occupants and stakeholders
4. Process – the activities that take place within the Place

This is particularly important for organisations that have a large campus or a large portfolio of real estate.

The facility manager's 4Ps – People, Place, Process, Plans

Table 2.1   A Facility Manager's 4P's: Plans, Place, People, Process.

4Ps	Description
Plans – Know where your organisation is headed	It is important to know the plans of your organisation. Examples of these plans include the following: Risk management plan, Marketing plan, Business plan, Master plan, Land use plan, Resource and staffing plan, Training and development plan. There are different time spans for plans. Some have a one-year outlook while others will be short-term, medium-term or long-term. For example, a budget is an example of an annual plan while a strategic plan

4Ps	Description
	is typically for a period of 5 to 10 years. A campus master plan can be for a period of 20 years. The plans typically have a revision cycle. For example, a new strategic plan would be created every 5 years and the plan would be reviewed annually. The facility manager has oversight over two key areas: operations and maintenance, planning and design. Operations and maintenance plans tend to be short-term in nature, typically one-year plans. The key long-term plan that a facility manager has oversight over is the facility master plan.
Place – Know your facility	Familiarising yourself with your facility is the first step. This can be done by studying the campus map that shows all the facilities and transport links. Following this, looking through the floor plans of the key buildings will aid in understanding what the major parts and spaces of the facility are. For facilities with large campuses, tools like Google Earth can be used to get an overview of the campus and see what the facility looks like from above.
People – Know your users and occupants	There is a need to know the organisation. This can be done by consulting the organisation chart that shows the names of the various people and their positions. There are different parts of an organisation, ranging from Operations, to Maintenance, Administration, etc. There are also users and occupants who are not part of your organisation. They also need to be considered.
Process – Know the activities	The facility manager has to understand what activities and processes take place within the facility he manages. For example, an airport processes passengers; there are arriving and departing passengers in an airport. In a university, there are education and research activities that are taking place.

Questions the FM needs to ask regarding the strategic plan

As the FM looks through the organisation's strategic plan, he has to consider the implications of the strategic plan on the physical facility and its operations. Here are some questions that he should ask:

1. Is the facility, in its current state, adequate to support the strategic plan?
2. Does the facility need to be expanded or renovated?
3. Where can I get the funding for the expansion or renovation of the facility?

Is the existing facility adequate?

The facility typically exists to support the business of the organisa-tion. As the organisation's strategy changes, the facility might need to change as well to align with the revised strategy. This change might be in terms of the size of the space or the quality of the space. Size could be determined in terms of floor area or floor to ceiling height. There might be new special requirements arising from the plan: for example, column-free space, floors that can take an increased load of new equipment, increased power requirements to support technology, or a higher level of aesthetics and architectural finish.

Does the facility need to be expanded or renovated?

Arising from the need for either a new purpose-built space or to adapt the existing space to meet the new requirements, the existing facility will have to be expanded or renovated. If this is the case, the require-ments must be put together, and a business case will have to be made for the facility expansion and or renovation. The relevant approving authority will have to agree to the project, and funding for the project has to be found.

Where can I get the funding for the expansion or renovation of the facility?

This question addresses the financial constraints the FM often finds that he is operating under. For organisations with a large portfolio of buildings, there is a constant need to renovate or rebuild facilities as the buildings age. Oftentimes, this is addressed through the annual capital improvement planning process where all the organisation's capital improvement requests are considered, and available capital finances allocated in the form of a capital budget. In addition to accumulated profits or surpluses, additional capital finances can be sought from investors or through the issuance of bonds or stocks depending on the type of organisation.

Other non-related questions

Are there any financial implications (from the FM's perspective) of the strategic plan? In addition to funding facility expansion and renovation, the implications of operating the space need to be considered.

Is additional manpower (in the FM department) needed to support the strategic plan? If additional manpower is needed, this will take some time to hire. An alternative would be the need to train existing manpower to support the new facility needs.

Example – Airport strategic plan

To put things into context, let us now look at the strategic plan in the context of an airport.

The parts of the airport strategic plan that need to be examined are the mission, vision, strategic goals and five-year priorities.

Table 2.2   Airport strategic plan of City X.

Mission
- We provide safe, secure, and efficient air transportation facilities and services that support and improve the quality of life and economic prosperity of City X.
Vision
- We will be widely-recognised as one of the best airports in the world.

Strategic Goals

- Economic vitality
- Customer service
- Operational efficiency and effectiveness
- Social responsibility
- Environmental stewardship

Five-year Priorities

1. Continue to develop a differentiated business strategy focused on quality service at a moderate cost.
2. Improve airport credit rating from A- to AA by December 2022.
3. Reduce the percentage of operating revenue paid by airlines to less than 40% by December 2022.
4. Secure non-stop long-haul transpacific air service to North America by December 2022.
5. Secure ISO 14000 certification for our Environmental Management System (EMS) by December 2022.

The mission, vision and objectives provide broad direction for the FM and his team regarding facilities. In this fictional airport strategic plan (Table 2.2), the emphasis should be on the five-year priorities that are well defined. Let us now review the list of five-year priorities and consider which ones have facility implications.

Priority 1 does not call out any specific facility need. However, whether this will have facility implications, will depend on the current service quality levels in the airport. If the facility is crowded and congested, there will be a need to build new facilities that will improve the service quality for users by increasing the area available and hence relieve the congestion. Quality service could also be in terms of amenities like restrooms and the availability of shops and services.

Priority 2 also has no specific facility implication. This priority is more for the finance division to work on.

Priority 3 has facility implications. In order to reduce airline contributions, there will be a need to increase facilities that generate non-airline revenue like retail shops, restaurants and parking facilities — as such, more commercial spaces need to be built in passenger terminals. In addition, commercially viable tracts of land on the airport can also be developed for hotels, shops and eateries. Another potential source of revenue are additional parking garages or parking lots that can be built to earn revenue for the airport.

For priority 4, the FM needs to consider the existing capacity of the Government Immigration and Customs facility. Can it accommodate the international passengers expected for this flight? If there is no such facility, one needs to be built in order for the Air Services Marketing team to be able to attract an airline to start such a route at the airport.

For priority 5, the FM needs to work together with the Environmental Manager to identify and address any facility shortcomings that might have implications on the ISO 14000 certification for the airport.

2.4 Essential #2b – Why the facility master plan should be aligned with the organisation's strategic plan

In the previous section, we looked at how the strategic plan drives the need for facilities. For large facilities, especially those with large land areas that are progressively developed, there will be a need for a facility master plan to guide the long-term development of the facility.

The **facility master plan** is one of the many plans that cascade from the strategic plan. Through a review of the organisation's vision, mission and strategic goals, a facility master plan is drawn up to support the organisation's strategic plan.

What is a facility master plan?

There are different names for a facility master plan, it is sometimes called a master plan or campus master plan. The master plan is drawn up with input from experts and stakeholders. Every community has values which are important to them and the master plan should reflect that.

The exact contents of the document will be dependent on the type of facility. At a minimum, the document will contain the following:

- Forecasts of space required
- Existing facilities and future facilities
- Phasing
- Codes and regulations
- Costs
- Environmental considerations

For large facilities like a university or an airport, master planning is a large undertaking that takes at least a year to complete because of the large amount of information that needs to be collected, large number of stakeholders that need to be consulted and multiple iterations that need to be considered before the master plan document is completed. The master planning process will be elaborated on in Chapter 6.

Example – The link between a university strategic plan and the university master plan

Let us now look at the link between a university strategic plan and a university master plan.

We will start out by examining the university strategic plan followed by the university master plan. In the context of the University of Texas at Austin (UT Austin), the strategic plan is embodied in the recommendations by the University's Commission of 125. The most recent UT Austin campus master plan was completed in 2013.

Every 25 years, UT Austin gathers a commission to examine how the University can best serve society for the next 25 years. The most recent commission, the Centennial Commission, gathered during the centennial of the founding of the University. In 2002, Commission of 125 was formed and two years later, they delivered their recommendations. In this example, the strategic plan guiding the university is the University's Commission of 125's report which contains two strategic initiatives and 16 recommendations. The 16 recommendations were grouped into four categories.

The first step for the FM is to look at each recommendation and see if there is a direct impact on facilities. The following five recommendations in two of the categories were most related to facilities.

Table 2.3   Five recommendations from the University of Texas at Austin (UT Austin)'s Commission of 125's report, 2013 relate to facilities.

Recommendations Five to Seven: Producing a Comprehensive Master Plan

Recommendation 5: Develop a University Master Plan to integrate academic planning and strategic goals with our facilities, infrastructure, and financial resources. The plan should be selective, and results should be measured systematically and objectively.

Recommendation 6: The University must consistently make the best use of its facilities, especially its classroom and laboratory space and off-campus properties, while maintaining a superior campus environment. New facilities should be designed and built more efficiently, with better coordination among academic, facilities planning, operations, and fundraising divisions.

Recommendation 7: Build financial strength and develop new public and private resources to support academic excellence.

Recommendations Eight to Thirteen: Creating Life-enhancing student learning experiences.

Recommendation 9: Increase the campus residence-hall capacity to 9,000 beds.

Recommendation 10: Construct student activity space on the east side or on the perimeter of the campus.

The second category of recommendations (Recommendations 5 to 7) called for a comprehensive master plan. Recommendation 5 explicitly calls out for a University Master Plan which will integrate strategic goals, facilities and financial resources.

Recommendation 6 emphasises the importance of having facilities that are well designed, well-built and well-used. Better coordination will translate into a better environment and better efficiency. Recommendation 7 is a focus on financial resources in order to realise the facility master plan.

The third category (Recommendations 8 to 13) addresses the student experience. Recommendations 9 and 10 are very explicit in terms of facilities. Recommendation 9 is focused on increasing the number of beds in the campus residence halls with a specific target of 9000 beds. Recommendation 10 is targeting student activity space with two possible options but has no specific target of area mentioned.

There are two specific district plans connected to the 2013 Campus Master Plan. The 2013 Campus Master Plan deals with all 430 acres of land in central Austin while the district plans deal with specific parts. The 2013 Medical District Master Plan focuses on 65 acres in the southeast portion of the campus while the 2015 East Campus Master Plan focuses on 52 acres of land on the eastern portion of the campus.

There is also the 2016 Texas Athletics Master Plan for Facility Improvements which deals with sports facilities on campus.

References

International Facility Management Association. (2009). *Strategic Facility Planning: A White Paper*. IFMA.

Mintzberg, H. (1994). *The rise and fall of strategic planning*. Prentice Hall.

Mintzberg, H. (2003). *The strategy process: concepts, contexts, cases*. Pearson education.

Transportation Research Board, Airport Cooperative Research Program. (2009). *ACRP Report 20: Strategic planning in the airport industry*. Transportation Research Board.

The University of Texas at Austin (2018), "Campus Master Plan", available at: http://campusplanning.utexas.edu/masterplan/ (assessed 22 May 2018)

The University of Texas at Austin (2018), "The Commission of 125", available at: http://sites.utexas.edu/commission-of-125/ (assessed 19 May 2018)

CHAPTER 3

The Owner's Role in Planning and Design

In this chapter, you will learn about the following:

1. Essential #3a – Responsibilities of the Owner's Representative (OwnerRep) during planning and design
2. The strategic brief
3. Essential #3b – Managing the selection process for design consultants
4. Evaluation criteria and weightage

Essential #3

Understand the responsibilities of the Owner's Representative during planning and design. Learn how to manage the selection process for design consultants.

In this chapter, we will be examining the role of the Owner's Representative (OwnerRep). For every building project undertaken in an organisation, there is a person that acts as the single point of contact for everything pertaining to that project. Typically, this person will be from the projects section of the facility management department of the owner organisation. The job title of this person varies from Project Manager to Facility Engineer to Project Coordinator.

For the purposes of this book, we will call this person the OwnerRep.

The three areas that will be studied in this chapter are the responsibilities of the OwnerRep, the strategic brief, and the selection of the consultant team. The proper oversight of the project by the OwnerRep, the writing of the strategic brief and the selection of the consultant team are three key tasks that need to be carried out by the OwnerRep for the successful development of the building.

3.1   Essential #3a – Responsibilities of the OwnerRep during planning and design

This section examines the responsibilities of the OwnerRep, the structure of the project management division of the organisation and the consultants that the OwnerRep will interact with.

The development of a building can be divided into the following phases:

- Planning Phase
- Design Phase
- Tendering Phase
- Construction Phase
- Post Construction Phase

Only the first three phases will be covered in this book as the construction and post-construction phases are not the focus of this book.

Let us use the example of a secondary school to illustrate what the OwnerRep does. The construction of a typical secondary school (25,000 to 30,000 square metres Gross Floor Area) takes about two years or less. The OwnerRep in this case would be from the Ministry of Education Planning and Engineering group.

The OwnerRep writes up the strategic brief in order to call a tender for consultant services for the design of the school building. This brief will include details like the site, parts of a secondary school (classrooms), and design guidelines. Once the brief is approved by the Board, a tender will be called for consultant services. The tender can be a single tender for multi-disciplinary services or individual tenders for each type of consultant service. The consultants provide design services which include designing the building, writing up the specifications, producing drawings and calling the tender for the construction of the building.

In Singapore, all Government Procurement Entities use an online procurement platform called GeBiz to call tenders for the procurement of goods and services. This includes consultant services and contractors for the construction of buildings. For consultant services tenders, the mode of tender evaluation is based on the price-quality method. In most construction tenders, the mode of tendering is based on price, where the lowest compliant tenderer wins the tender and gets the construction project.

Responsibilities across all phases of the project

From the inception of the project in the planning phase, through the design and construction phases, the OwnerRep has the following responsibilities:

- Represents the interests of the owner and users.
  - o Acts as the channel for all official information being given to consultants and contractors.
  - o Typically have other staff from the Owner organisation in the project team to provide input to the design and construction process.
- Ensures that there is funding for the project. Sometimes from grants.
- Manage the design consultants.
  - o Attend project meetings (typically weekly). These meetings have a lot of people attending.
  - o Gets information for the consultants from Owner organisation.
  - o Ensure that submissions (e.g. drawings) are reviewed and comments are returned in a timely manner.

Responsibilities at each phase of the project

For each phase, there are additional responsibilities which are carried out by the OwnerRep. The description of specific tasks for the planning, design and tendering phases are elaborated upon in the following table.

Table 3.1   The five project phases and their associated responsibilities.

	Phase	Description of Tasks
1	Planning	Budget preparation - Get project in the Capital improvement plan and funded - Prepare spending plans Design consultant services - Prepare Design Consultant Services document - Evaluate submissions and select consultant - Prepare Approval paper to Management and Board (internal approval process) - Review and approve proposed schedules - Coordinate project design input from appropriate Owner personnel and tenants - Document and involve all stakeholders
2	Design	- Attend design progress and review meetings - Coordinate project input from appropriate Owner personnel and tenants (scope, purpose, background, existing conditions, restrictions and controls, etc.) - Monitor Owner staff input to ensure proper development of project scope (prevent scope creep) - Sign off monthly invoices or pay milestone payments

	Phase	Description of Tasks
3	Tendering	- Ensure that cost estimate (by Consultant QS) is within available budget prior to calling for contractor tender. If insufficient, modify scope or available funding as appropriate - Participate in tender briefing - Assist in preparation of responses to tender questions and addenda, review and approve addenda - Assist in review and acceptance of tender price and tender options - Assist in preparation and presentation of Approval Paper to Management and Board (if required)
4	Construction	The Construction phase will not be elaborated on as it is not the focus of this book.
5	Post-Construction	The Post-Construction phase will not be elaborated on as it is not the focus of this book.

The project management division in the owner organisation

Some organisations are asset-heavy and have a large portfolio of facilities. These organisations, like universities and airports, tend to have a project management division. For smaller organisations that do not have full-time project management staff, this function is normally outsourced to a consultant for the duration of the project.

The size of the project management division depends on the size of the organisation, the number and scale of projects that are being managed, and the extent to which projects are managed in-house.

For a facility like a medium hub airport, the division can be organised as shown in the following figure.

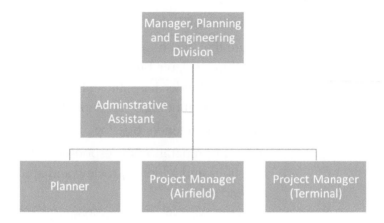

Fig. 3.1   Org chart of a typical project management division.

There is a manager that oversees the division, and a facility planner and project managers for different assets. For example, one of the project managers could be responsible for the airfield, another for passenger terminal and building projects, and another to oversee tenant renovations. When the facility is sufficiently large or has a lot of expansion work, it can support a full-time facility planner.

When there are a lot of large projects happening at the facility, the project management division becomes very large and will report directly to the Chief Executive Officer (CEO). For example, when there is a huge project like a new airport terminal building, there will be a large project management team spending hundreds of millions of dollars.

The organisation chart evolves as the needs of the organisation change. The project management division scales up when there is a very large development and scales back down after the development finishes.

Who are the consultants involved in the design of the building?

The OwnerRep will interact with a number of consultants during the design phase of the project. It is a team effort. Each consultant could be from a different company or the same company. On large or specialised projects, there are also specialist consultants providing services for specific aspects of the project; e.g. landscape consultant, acoustic consultant, façade consultant, etc.

A typical project will have a number of consultants involved in the design process as shown in the following table.

Table 3.2 List of consultants typically involved in the design process of a building and their roles.

	Consultant	Role
1	Architect	Leads the building team, develops ideas and concepts for the building. Responsible for ensuring that the building meets the applicable development control regulations, regulatory and technical requirements. Selects materials, ensures functionality, aesthetics.
2	Civil and Structural Engineer	Designs the structural system. Determines the sizing of columns and beams in a building. Designs a practical and safe structure to withstand environment.
3	Mechanical and Electrical Engineer	Designs the services in the building: electrical, lighting, air conditioning, ventilation. Creates a comfortable working environment for occupants.
4	Quantity Surveyor	Manages the cost of the building project. Administers tenders and contracts.

3.2 The strategic brief

Since most owners do not continuously build new buildings, they choose not to do design work in-house. Instead this work is outsourced to consultants who are engaged to do the necessary design work. The main purpose of the strategic brief is to communicate the Owner's requirements and expectations to these consultants.

For the purposes of this book, I have chosen to call the initial document issued by the owner to their consultants the 'Strategic Brief'. The strategic brief may also be called 'employer's requirements'.

This strategic brief may be further worked and elaborated on by the architect and consultants during the design phase. For the purposes of this book and to distinguish it from the initial document produced by the Owner, I will be using the term "Program" to refer to this document when the programming process is elaborated on in Chapter 5.

There is no standard strategic brief, as strategic briefs vary in terms of document length and depth of detail. It is dependent on the norms of the owner organisation, and detailing it out to the maximum extent possible is important to reduce contractual issues and disputes that might arise later. The recipients of the strategic brief are the consultants interested in working on the project. They will prepare a proposal in response to the Request for Design Consultancy Services.

The contents of a strategic brief are as follows:

• Background information; e.g. Project objectives
• Project description; e.g. site location
• Requirements; e.g. Design principles, Sustainability requirements
• Timeline (schedule) of works and deliverables
• Estimated Project cost
• Services required (or scope of services)
• Information provided by Employer

Background information, project description

Background information

• The project objectives help parties involved understand the motivation behind the project and what the Owner would like to accomplish.

Project description

- This will be in terms of the site and the building to be built.
- The site location will be provided with the site area in terms of hectares.
- For the building(s) that need to built, the estimated gross floor area of the building(s) is typically provided.
- If the building is made up of units like beds in a hospital, or number of classrooms in a school, this number is also provided.

Requirements

Before designing the building, it is important to understand what the users require from the building. At the most basic level, the users of a facility are those that occupy the building. They could be workers that work full-time in the building or visitors that occasionally visit the building as customers or service providers. The organisation that owns or rents the building is also considered a user.

The requirements need to be translated into written form and organised so that they can be communicated to the architect and the design team. Data to support the requirements are also collected at this point. Requirements can be divided into two categories: functional requirements and technical requirements.

- Functional requirements
  - Analyse operations
  - Take into account activities that take place in the facility
  - Consider the type and amount of space needed
- Technical requirements
  - Technical standards
  - Industry standards and guidelines

Establishing space requirements

- Step 1 –   Identify the type of activities to be accommodated in the planned development within the planning horizon (typically five years long).

- Step 2 – Establish the basis for the space needed. i.e. conduct technical analysis/define spatial characteristics. Collect inputs from the users and occupants via interviews and questionnaires.

- Step 3 – Set space standards depending on facility type (reference *The Metric Handbook*, to familiarise with a specific facility type). This will depend on architectural and engineering design standards, building code regulations.

- Step 4 – Calculate space requirements required for the activities and the organisation.

For small facilities, this collection of requirements will be the job of the facility manager who is most aware of the problems in the facility. Usually, as a facility gets bigger, dedicated space planners are engaged. For very large projects, there are committees with representatives from all the end-user groups.

How to collect requirements

- Look at similar buildings
- Get users to draw up their needs
- Collection of data through surveys

Timeline of works and estimated project cost

Timeline

- An estimated timeline (schedule) should be provided to the consultants as this helps them in planning resources necessary for the project, which in turn affects the pricing of the consultant fees. For example, a project that is needed urgently would have a shortened timeline. This would affect the amount of resources required and the time-period during which they are needed.

Estimated project cost

- An estimated project cost or budgetary estimate provides a sense of scale of the project for the consultants. This provides the consultant with a basis of estimating the consultant fee for the project as the fee is typically expressed in terms of a percentage of the total project cost.

Scope of services and information provided by employer

Scope of services

- There is a need to define the scope of services required from the consultants. For example, architectural design services, civil and structural design services, mechanical and electrical services, cost estimating services, tendering services, or contract administration services.

Information provided by the Employer

- If the Owner has information that is available, this can be stated up front so that the consultants are aware of it. This could potentially reduce the amount of preparatory work that the consultants need to do and reduce the chargeable hours for the project.

- Examples of this information could be past design studies, building programming reports, site investigation reports, etc.

3.3 Essential #3b – Managing the selection process for design consultants

The second key task that the OwnerRep has to do is to oversee the appointment of the design consultants. This is a critical step as the success of the project hinges on the appointment of suitable consultants to advance the design process as well as to oversee the construction of the new building.

The selection process

So how are design consultants selected? These are the steps in the selection process for consultants:

1. Write the strategic brief
2. Compile the tender document

3. Issue the tender documents
4. Evaluate the submissions by potential consultants
5. Seek approval
6. Appoint the most suitable consultant

Step 1 – Write up the strategic brief

The first step is to write up the strategic brief. The strategic brief encapsulates the requirements of the Owner for the project. This was covered in detail in Section 3.2. The main purpose is to communicate to the potential design consultants what is important to the Owner for the project. The strategic brief, together with the relevant administrative documents (tendering requirements, conditions of contract, etc.), are compiled in a tender document.

Step 2 – Issue the request for consultancy services

The second step is to issue the request for consultancy services document to interested parties. There is a tender briefing to explain the Owner's requirements and answer any questions that the tenderers might have. Proposals prepared in accordance to the Owner's format and requirements are submitted by the tender closing date.

Step 3 – Evaluate the submitted proposals

The third step is to evaluate the submitted proposals. The submitted proposals are first checked to ensure that all the required submissions are present. In many countries including Singapore, the Quality Fee Method (QFM) is used. The tenderer submits 'two envelopes', one containing the technical proposal (qualifications of the firm) and another containing the financial proposal. To ensure that price does not influence the evaluation of the technical proposal, the technical proposal is first evaluated and scored before the financial proposal is opened and scored. The two scores are combined and the proposal with the highest score is awarded the job. For larger projects, there are interviews for the top few tenderers. An interview score can be given and taken into account for the selection of the most suitable tenderer.

In some countries like the United States, government-issued requests for consultancy services typically only require the submission of qualifications. The fee proposal is not required at the initial submission stage. The evaluation is qualifications-based. After the selection of the most qualified tenderer, a fee proposal is requested and checked that it is reasonable and fair. For areas where there is disagreement, there is a negotiation with the most qualified tenderer. In the event that the negotiations fail, the next most qualified tenderer is invited to submit a fee proposal. Once there is an agreement on the fee proposal, the next step is to get approval for the award of the tender.

Step 4 – Submit recommendation for approval and award to successful tenderer

The fourth step is for the evaluation committee to submit a recommendation for approval to the relevant approving authorities. The approving authority will vary according to the value of the consultancy services. The OwnerRep will have to shepherd this process. Once approval is given, the tender can be awarded with the signing of the contract by the Owner and the tenderer. The appointed consultant can then commence work on the project.

3.4 Evaluation criteria for consultant and weightage

As mentioned earlier, the submissions need to be evaluated according to a set of criteria. These criteria should be pre-determined before the submissions are evaluated in order to ensure fair play. Some owners might opt to have standardised criteria for all projects while others might choose to vary them according to the needs of different projects.

List of criteria

Each criterion covers an area that is important to the owner. Each of the selected criterion needs to be assigned a certain weightage according to its level of importance relative to the others.

The following are standard criteria that can be used for evaluating consultant submissions. They can be grouped into three categories that need to be considered: Organisation, Experience, Others.

- Organisation
  - Structure of Project Team
  - Approach to Project

- Experience
  - Lead company's comparable project experience
  - Major scopes of work with comparable project experience
  - Experience of Project Manager
  - Experience of Principal

- Others
  - Team's experience with local issues
  - Client's experience with Prime

The first category to be considered is organisation, where the structure of the project team is considered. The consultant project team is typically made up of more than one consultant, so it is important to consider how they are organised. Equally important is how they intend to approach the project and their methodology for the various phases of the project, particularly the design phase. The company should have a good team assembled and a suitable methodology to complete the project successfully.

The second category to be considered is the experience of the key staff and the companies in the consultant team. The resumes of the key staff (Project Manager, Principal–Lead design staff) provided in the tender submission will be reviewed by the evaluation committee for relevant experience. The companies should have a good track record and should have completed similar projects in terms of type and scale.

The third category to be considered are other issues that are important to the Owner. For example, whether the companies are familiar with the local environment and the owner's previous experience with the companies.

Weightage

Next, we consider the possible weightage for each criterion. The following is an example of possible weightages that can be assigned to each criterion for tenders that only consider the 'Quality' of the submitted proposal and where the fee is negotiated.

Table 3.3　Example of a list of evaluation criteria and the possible weightages assigned to each criterion.

SNo	Evaluation Criteria	Weightage
1	Structure of Project Team	10
2	Approach to Project	20
3	Experience of Project Manager	12
4	Experience of Principal	8
5	Lead company's comparable project experience	15
6	Major scopes of work comparable project experience	15
7	Team's experience with local issues	10
8	Client's experience with Prime	10
	Sub-total	**100**
9	Interview (if applicable)	15
	Total	**115**

Items 1 to 8 add up to a score of 100. Item 9 shows an optional interview that the Owner may choose to have with the top two or three consultant teams (in terms of scores).

For the above example, it can be seen that items 1 and 2 (Organisation) add up to 30% of the score or about one-third. Items 3 to 6 (Experience) add up to 50% or half of the score. While items 7 and 8 (Others) relate to other issues important to the Owner and account for 20% or one-fifth of the score.

Quality-fee weightage

In many instances, the consultant team's fee is often a key consideration of the evaluation. For example, in Singapore, in the standard evaluation criteria, the quality of the consultant's proposal takes up 70% of the weightage, and the consultant's fee accounts for 30%. This can be varied according to the projects' needs. For example, 'quality' can be 80% and 'fee' 20% for projects that are more complex and where the consultant's qualifications are more critical.

Evaluation committee and approval of selection

For every tender, there is an evaluation committee that is formed for that particular tender. Typically, each member of the committee reviews all the submitted proposals individually and assigns a score to them. This is followed by an evaluation committee meeting where all the members combine their scores to produce a ranked list (according to the scores) of the most qualified tenderer.

Once the evaluation is completed, a tender recommendation report needs to be submitted to the approvals board. The following information needs to be in the tender recommendation:

- Need for the project and the description of the proposed project
- Name of the recommended consultant/consultant team
- List of consultant teams in terms of their ranking starting from the team that has the highest score. A matrix with a breakdown of each team's score in each category is also provided as backup material.
- The fourth item is the availability of funds for the consultancy services and which fund or budget it is coming from.

The recommendation goes before the approval board at their regularly scheduled meetings. This is an opportunity for the board or those present to ask questions or seek clarification. The board can choose to approve, reject or defer the recommendation provided.

References

Blyth, A., & Worthington, J. (2010). *Managing the brief for better design*. Routledge.

Brauer, R. L. (1992). *Facilities planning: The user requirements method*. American Management Association.

Building Control Authority (2018), "Quality Fee Method", available at: https://www.bca.gov.sg/QFM/qfm.html (accessed 12 Jul 2018)

Building Control Authority (2018), "Public Sector Panels of Consultants", available at: https://www.bca.gov.sg/PanelsConsultants/panels_consultants.html (accessed 24 Jul 2018)

Building Control Authority (2018), "The six professionals in the construction value chain", available at: https://www.youtube.com/watch?v=chl5_z-gkWg (accessed 24 Jul 2018)

Chartered Institute of Building (2014). *Code of practice for project management for construction and development*. Wiley Blackwell.

de Jong, T. M., & Van Der Voordt, D. J. M. (Eds.). (2002). *Ways to study and research: urban, architectural, and technical design*. Ios Press.

Littlefield, D. (2012). *Metric handbook*. Routledge.

Rondeau, E. P., Brown, R. K., & Lapides, P. D. (2012). *Facility management*. John Wiley & Sons.

Roper, K., & Payant, R. (2014). *The facility management handbook*. Amacom.

CHAPTER 4

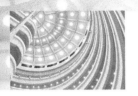

Space Standards and Universal Design

In this chapter, you will learn about the following:

1. Essential #4a – Space and humans — Recognising how occupants and their activities impact the size and design of a space

2. People with disabilities

3. Essential #4b – Universal Design — Making spaces accessible to all

4. Essential #4c – Area definitions and measurement methods

5. Essential #4d – Space standards

Essential #4

Recognise how occupants and their activities impact the size and design of a space. Learn about universal design, area definitions and space standards.

This chapter explores the space requirements of humans, universal design, area definitions and space standards.

The first section looks at the space requirements of humans. At the heart of facilities planning is space; how to plan and design the space — the dimensions, layout, and quality of the space. The amount of space required is determined by the area occupied by the dimensions of the people using the space and the dimensions of the furniture and equipment that need to be in that space.

The second section considers the space requirements of people with disabilities. This is followed by the third section that considers the principles of Universal Design and how to make the spaces in the built environment accessible to all types of people, varying in abilities, age and size.

The fourth section considers how space is measured, specifically area definitions. The fifth section considers space standards. For each building type, there are space standards that are either legislated norms or industry norms which may vary from jurisdiction to jurisdiction.

4.1 Essential #4a – Space and humans — Recognising how occupants and their activities impact the size and design of a space

At the most fundamental level, the size of the human occupants and their activities determine the size of a space. Hence, it is important to have a basic understanding of the measurements of the human body and the spatial requirements of humans in different situations.

Anthropometrics studies the "metrics" or measurements of the human body. When designing an interior space, it is necessary to consider the variety of users and their varying sizes. This section offers a basic introduction to anthropometrics by examining the measurements of adults.

The following books are useful references for the planning and design of buildings. They are useful sources of human body measurements, space requirements of humans in different situations, space standards and the considerations for different types of buildings:

- *The Metric Handbook*, 5th edition, 2015
- *Neufert Architects' data*, 4th edition, 2012

The Metric Handbook is a useful reference that can be used when designing a building type that you are unfamiliar with. However, it must be remembered that it is written from a British point of view and based on the average dimensions for British adults. It is necessary to adapt the measurements and standards for the local environment.

Adults

The measurements for an adult in various positions need to be considered. Examples of the various positions are:

- Standing
- Sitting on the floor
- Sitting on a chair at a table
- Lying down
- Kneeling
- Squatting

The dimensions of standing adults and sitting adults will be examined to introduce the concept to readers. A more detailed treatment of the subject can be found in architectural standards books like the two mentioned above.

Dimensions of standing adults

As an example, let us consider a standing adult.

The measurements in the vertical dimension that need to be considered are:

- Height
  - From the ground to the top of the head
  - From the ground to the eye level
  - From the ground to the shoulder level
  - From the ground to the hand level (when hands are placed on the side of the body)

The measurements in the horizontal dimension (in terms of width) that need to be considered are:

- Width (of the body)
  - at shoulders
  - at hip

In terms of space occupied by a standing adult, the average British male is 174 cm tall, and has a shoulder width of 46.5 cm. The average British female is 161 cm tall and has a shoulder width of 39.5 cm.

As a comparison, in an anthropometric study of Singaporean university students conducted in 2010, the average height of a male was 174 cm tall and that of a female was 162 cm. The study compared the data collected with another study conducted in 1990 and it was found that the average heights of males and females had increased by 5 cm and 6.85 cm respectively.

Another dimension that needs to be considered is the reach of a human. For example, are they able to reach the switches in the room? Measurements for reach include the following:

- Forward arm reach
- Arm span (with the arms stretched out sideways)
- One pace (or step)

The average British male is able to reach 78 cm forward, and the average British female is able to reach 70.5 cm forward. With arms raised, the span of the average British male is 179 cm, while the average British female's arm span is 160.5 cm. One pace of the average British male is 72 cm while that of the female is 62 cm.

Dimensions of sitting adults

It is also important to examine the dimensions of adults in the sitting position as this drives the dimensions of the furniture, such as tables and chairs, in the room.

In the vertical dimension, the following dimensions need to be considered:

- Seat to top of head (sitting height)
- Seat to eye level
- Seat to shoulder level
- Seat to elbow level

- Floor to seat level
- Floor to top of thigh

The following are horizontal dimensions that need to be considered:

- Back to heel of foot
- Back to front of calf

The average British male has a sitting height of 91 cm while the average British female has a sitting height of 85 cm. The floor to seat level for the average British male and female are 44 cm and 40 cm respectively.

Moving humans (adults) – Corridor widths

Having considered the space that people require when they are stationary, let us now consider the space required when they are moving by considering corridor widths.

For one person, the following minimum corridor widths (wall to wall) are suggested:

- One person walking sideways 350 mm
- One person walking 575 mm
- One person walking with occasional passing 900 mm

You will notice that the width varies depending on the how the person walks, whether sideways or normally. It is also increased if space is required for passing.

For the design of corridors, the following widths (wall to wall) are suggested (with 10% extra to allow for movement):

- One person; 625 mm
- Two persons; 1150 mm
- Three persons; 1700 mm
- Four persons; 2250 mm

For fire safety reasons, there is normally a legally prescribed minimum corridor width. However, the corridor widths tend to be wider than the minimum for the comfort of occupants and based on the facility's needs.

4.2 People with disabilities

A proportion of any country's population are disabled at any one time. In the United States, 19% of population is reported to have a disability, with half of them having a severe disability. Included in this group are people who might be temporarily disabled as a result of an injury, and that need mobility assistance (e.g. to be in wheelchairs) while their bodies are recovering. The reach of people with disabilities is also different from normal adults.

People in wheelchairs

Let us now consider people with disabilities who require the use of a wheelchair to move around. The following are some of the dimensions that need to be considered for people in wheelchairs:

- Vertical dimensions
  - Height
  - Eye level (from ground)
  - Shoulder level (from ground)
  - Hand level (from ground)

- Horizontal dimensions
  - Width of wheelchair

- Reach
  - Forward arm reach

For example, the height of a British adult female in a wheelchair is 125.5 cm, with an eye level of 115.5 cm from the ground. Her forward arm reach is 49.5 cm.

Corridor widths and ramp gradients (for people moving around in wheelchairs)

To ensure that people with disabilities in wheelchairs are able to navigate the built environment, two examples of considerations are corridor widths and ramp gradients.

In terms of movement for people in wheelchairs, the minimum width for a corridor that has wheelchair traffic is 760 mm. However, for ease of movement, the recommended width is 900 mm. If the wheelchair user is assisted by someone pushing, the recommended width can be reduced to 800 mm. If there is a requirement for two wheelchairs (with assistants) to pass one another, the recommended width is 1700 mm.

Where there are steps and changes in level, there needs to be ramps to accommodate people in wheelchairs. One of the key concerns for ramps for people in wheelchairs is the gradient of the ramps. A typical gradient for ramps is 1:12 (or 8.3%). Reference needs to be made to the local code of accessibility standard for actual requirements in that jurisdiction.

4.3   Essential #4b – Universal Design — Making spaces accessible to all

According to Ronald Mace, "Universal Design is the design of products and environment to be usable by all people, to the greatest extent possible, without the need for adaptation or specialised design."

There is a need to design for all people and cater for the whole range of different human needs. Different people have varying levels of physical abilities. This is also the case for cognitive abilities. Universal Design allows all people-types to move around independently with minimal assistance, allowing them to participate fully in mainstream daily life.

The Centre for Universal Design at North State University suggests Seven Principles of Universal Design. They are:

1. Equitable Use
2. Flexibility in Use

3. Simple and Intuitive
4. Perceptible Information
5. Tolerance for Error
6. Low Physical Effort
7. Size and Space for Approach and Use

There are people with varying abilities that need to navigate the built environment. Examples of these people are:

- People in wheelchairs
- Visually Impaired
- Hearing Impaired
- Elderly
- Pregnant women
- Young children
- People with temporary disabilities

People in wheelchairs need a relatively flat surface to move from place to place. The floor needs to be kerb-free and should have minimal sloping surfaces in order for wheelchair users to move around unassisted. Openings need to be sufficiently large enough for the wheelchair user to move through. Doors ideally should be automatic or should be designed in such a way that the wheelchair user is able to open and close them easily. Lifts or ramps need to be provided for changes in level.

People in wheelchairs are in a seated position and have a more limited span of reach. For example, lift buttons and light switches need to be low enough for a person in a wheelchair to reach. For service counters at offices and shops, counters need to be sufficiently low enough to serve customers in wheelchairs. Facilities such as accessible toilets need to be provided.

Consideration also needs to be given to how people in wheelchairs get to and from buildings. There needs to be provision of accessible parking spaces. Connections to public transport (transit stations and bus stops) also need to be accessible to people in wheelchairs.

For the visually impaired, the provision of a level surface with minimum barriers is vital. For heavily trafficked paths, tactile paving can be provided to guide visually impaired persons. This is common in rail stations and transport interchanges. Lift buttons with Braille and floor announcements are helpful add-ons in buildings.

Elderly with reduced mobility and strength will also find level surfaces and minimum barriers helpful. In addition, providing seating or resting areas on long paths or intermediate landings on long flights of stairs should be part of buildings that have elderly users. Grab rails on the side of stairs will help elderly with limited strength climb them. Grab rails in toilet cubicles are also necessary for buildings frequented by the elderly. Pregnant women may also experience reduced mobility and strength, and enhancements typically for elderly would also be helpful for them.

For facilities that have young children as users, the following provisions need to be made. In terms of movement, stairs railings appropriate for their height should be provided. Age-appropriate furniture and toilet fittings is another provision. For shopping centres that would like to attract families with young children, designated parking for vehicles with young children can be provided. There should also be consideration for the easy movement of strollers.

Code on accessibility in the built environment

To accelerate the implementation of accessibility provisions in the built environment, legislation has been introduced to make a minimum standard mandatory. Legislation had previously been focused on making buildings accessible to people in wheelchairs. This has since expanded to include more universal design provisions.

An example of legislation is the Singapore Building and Construction Authority (BCA)'s "Code on Accessibility in the Built Environment" that building owners, introduced in 1990. All new buildings built since then have to comply with the Code of Accessibility in the Built Environment. Starting from 2017, BCA introduced mandatory requirements for existing commercial and institutional buildings. An accessibility fund has also been established to assist building owners with upgrading their buildings.

In addition, BCA also publishes a "Universal Design Guide" and gives out awards to encourage building owners to incorporate Universal Design into their developments.

4.4 Essential #4c – Area definitions and measurement methods

One of the ways that space is measured is in terms of area. Areas are measured in terms of square metres (metric) or square feet (Imperial/ English system).

We will be looking at the definitions of different terms relating to area, how they are measured and building efficiency factors.

Different definitions and measures for different purposes

The definition of building area and its measurements varies with the intention of the people (e.g. architects, facility managers) using the definition and measures.

The floor area of a building is needed for various reasons. Examples include:

- Development permission – calculating the area to abide by the permissible plot ratio under zoning regulations. For example, the Singapore Urban Redevelopment Authority (URA) defines gross floor area for the purposes of calculating plot ratio for planning control and calculation of the development charge.
- Tax purposes – Property tax is collected based on the floor area of a building, according to building use/construction type.
- Cost estimating – at the beginning stages of the project, there is not much design detail available, so cost estimates are done on per unit area basis according to building use/construction type.
- Data collection – buildings are of varying sizes, so a useful unit to compare across different building sizes is 'per square metre'.

Definitions of different areas (gross floor area and net floor area)

We will now be examining the definition of Gross Floor Area and Net Floor Area.

The 'Gross Floor Area' of a building is the total area of all the covered spaces in the building. The following is an example of a definition of gross floor area. The URA, Singapore's planning authority, defines "Gross Floor Area" as:

- "All covered floor areas of a building, except otherwise exempted, and uncovered areas for commercial uses are deemed the gross floor area of the building for purposes of plot ratio control and development charge. The gross floor area is the total area of the covered floor space measured between the centre line of party walls, including the thickness of external walls but excluding voids."

The gross floor area of a building can be divided into respective areas. For the ease of illustration, let us consider a typical floor in a multi-storey office building. The following are the spaces on a typical floor:

- Office space: There are various rooms in the offices. Examples of these would include individual offices, shared offices, meeting rooms, storage rooms.
- Horizontal circulation: Corridors between the office space, restrooms, mechanical and electrical rooms, lifts and staircases.
- Restrooms.
- Mechanical and electrical rooms.
- Vertical circulation: Lifts and staircases.

The 'Net Floor Area' is derived by adding up the office space. It is primarily the area occupied by the office staff and does not include the other spaces mentioned above.

There is a need to read the fine print when looking at definitions of areas. An example of standardisation is the International Property Measurement Standards (IPMS) that are published by an international coalition of property-related organisations. IPMS 1 applies for all buildings and is used for measuring the total area of a building. IPMS 2 is focused on the categorisation of internal spaces. IPMS 3 is used to measure the areas that are occupied exclusively by an occupier (or tenant) versus shared facilities.

Building efficiency factors

The building efficiency factor is the 'Net Floor Area' divided by the 'Gross Floor Area'. A typical office building has a building efficiency factor of 60 to 70%. It is useful to compare similar buildings that serve the same function. This ensures that the usable space in the buildings are maximised and the adequate ratios are maintained. For example, are there corridors that are not needed? Is the layout of each floor optimised to maximise rentable area for the owner?

Different building types have different efficiency factors. This difference can be accounted for by the amount of internal partitions and circulation spaces. Let us consider the difference between office buildings versus warehouses. For example, a warehouse has a very high efficiency factor compared to an office building because a warehouse has very few internal partitions and circulation spaces. Another reason could be the presence of larger mechanical rooms because of special needs. For example, a research building might have need for more cooling or ventilation or require additional fire suppression equipment.

4.5   Essential #4d – Space standards

How much space is needed for an office with 20 persons? How much space is needed for a lecture theatre with 200 students? Space standards are needed to define the space requirements for different use types.

An example of a space standard is the number of square metres (m^2) needed per person in that space. The area of the room is determined by multiplying the number of people occupying the room multiplied by the space required by each person in that particular setting.

For an office with 20 persons with a space standard of 10 m² per employee, the required floor area will be 200 m².

For a lecture theatre with 200 students and a space standard of 1.5 m² per student, the required floor area will be 300 m².

Example: Airport space standards

Let us consider space standards in the context of airports. In addition to the usual building space standards, airport space standards have to consider the size of aircraft.

When designing airports, a unique consideration is the space requirements of aircraft. Based on forecasts, the airport will select a 'design aircraft' to base their airfield design and passenger terminal design on.

For the airfield, which includes the runway(s) and taxiways, the 'design aircraft' selected would normally be the largest aircraft type that is expected to operate regularly at the airport. The length, wingspan and turning radius of the aircraft have to be carefully considered.

The aircraft parking stands will be designed around the aircraft fleet mix expected at the airport. The critical dimensions would be the length and wingspan of the aircraft. An example of a space standard would be the minimum wingtip to wingtip separation distance that is required between aircraft for safety reasons. The International Civil Aviation Organisation (ICAO), the United Nations Agency for Civil Aviation, recommends a clearance of 3 m for Code A and B aircraft, 4.5 m for Code C aircraft, and 7.5 m for Code D, E and F aircraft. Generally, Code A aircraft are the smallest in size and Code F aircraft are the largest.

Example: Airport passenger terminal space standards

There are also unique standards for the airport passenger terminal building. Key standards for airport development are found in the Airport Development Reference Manual (ADRM) published by the International Air Transport Association (IATA), the trade association that represents most of the airlines of the world.

Space standards can be found in the ADRM. The following are examples of space standards for the key areas that passengers flow through when departing from the airport:

- Public Departure Hall – 2.0 to 2.3 m^2 per passenger
- Check-in – 1.3 to 1.8 m^2 per passenger
- Security Control – 1.0 to 1.2 m^2 per passenger

Let us consider the differences in the space standards in the above-mentioned areas.

The public departure hall has the largest space requirement as there is a lot of movement of people with their baggage, often with baggage trolleys. They are also accompanied by well-wishers sending them off.

The check-in area does not require as much space because there is less movement compared to the public departure hall so there is a reduction in the space requirement. The divestment of baggage and checked-in items occurs at this point.

At security control, passengers no longer have their baggage with them, so the space requirements reduce further. At this point, only passengers are allowed in the security area and well-wishers are not allowed to proceed into this area.

References

Ashford, N. J., Mumayiz, S., & Wright, P. H. (2011). *Airport engineering: planning, design, and development of 21st century airports.* John Wiley & Sons.

Building and Construction Authority (2013). "Code on accessibility in the built environment", available at: https://www.bca.gov.sg/BarrierFree/others/ACCESSIBILITY_CODE_2013.pdf (accessed 4 Aug 2018)

Building and Construction Authority (2016). *Universal Design Guidelines.* Singapore.

Building and Construction Authority (2016). "BCA to expand accessibility mandatory requirements for existing buildings" available at: https://www.bca.gov.sg/newsroom/others/SUDW_Media_Release_270716.pdf (accessed 4 Aug 2018)

Buxton, P. (Ed.). (2015). *Metric handbook: planning and design data.* Routledge.

Chuan, T. K., Hartono, M., & Kumar, N. (2010). Anthropometry of the Singaporean and Indonesian populations. *International Journal of Industrial Ergonomics, 40*(6), 757–766.

International Air Transport Association (2017). "Improved level of service concept", available at: https://www.iata.org/services/consulting/Documents/cons-apcs-los-handout.pdf (accessed 6 Aug 2018)

International Property Measurement Standards Coalition (2018). "The Standards", available at: https://ipmsc.org/standards/ (accessed 1 Aug 2018)

Knight Frank Singapore (2018). "Space requirement and renovation cost", available at: http://www.knightfrank.com.sg/resources/pdfs/space-requirement-renovation-cost.pdf (accessed 6 Aug 2018)

Neufert, E., Neufert, P., & Kister, J. (2012). *Architects' data.* John Wiley & Sons.

Nussbaumer, L. L. (2014). *Human factors in the built environment.* Bloomsbury Publishing USA.

Transportation Research Board, Airport Cooperative Research Program (2010). *ACRP Report 25: Airport Passenger Terminal Planning and Design, Volume 1: Guidebook.* Transportation Research Board.

United States Census Bureau (2012). "Nearly 1 in 5 people have a disability in the U.S.", available at: https://www.census.gov/newsroom/releases/archives/miscellaneous/cb12-134.html (accessed 3 Aug 2018)

Urban Redevelopment Authority (2018). "Development Control – Gross Floor Area Handbook", available at: https://www.ura.gov.sg/Corporate/Guidelines/Development-Control/gross-floor-area (accessed 31 Jul 2018)

CHAPTER 5

Programming and Site Selection

In this chapter, you will learn about the following:

1. What is "programming of buildings"?
2. Essential #5a – Learning the process for programming building spaces
3. Programmatic concepts
4. Essential #5b – The site selection process
5. Site evaluation criteria

Essential #5

Learn the process for programming building spaces and how to select a site for development.

In an earlier chapter, we looked at various phases of the planning and design of a building project. After the scoping and feasibility phases are completed, the owner provides the architect with a strategic brief. This strategic brief is further developed and expanded on before the schematic design phase commences. This process of expanding the strategic brief is known as "Programming" in United States, where it has evolved into a very structured process. This chapter provides a basic introduction to programming and includes a list of references for further reading for those that wish to delve deeper.

To complete the picture, the site selection process and possible criteria to use are also covered in this chapter.

The facility management staff that are responsible for planning and design need to have a good understanding of these two processes as the consultants might not be on board to assist in the early stages of the development of the building project.

5.1 What is "programming of buildings"?

The programming of buildings is sometimes referred to as Architectural Programming. In countries that are part of the British Commonwealth, this process is also known as briefing. The desired end of the programming process is to have a "program of requirements".

I will be using the American spelling of "program" for this chapter as the British spelling of "programme" is typically used to refer to a schedule dealing with time.

According to the American Institute of Architects (2000), programming is "the thorough and systematic evaluation of the interrelated values, goals, facts and needs of a client's organisation, facility users, and the surrounding community. A well-conceived program leads to high-quality design."

In my view, programming straddles the planning and design stages of the development of a building. As mentioned previously, planning consists of the scoping and feasibility stages. As part of the planning process, it is often necessary do some programming of the building in order to communicate the scope of the work to the consultants that are engaged to design the building.

The program is updated and added to at different points of the planning and design process. Blyth & Worthington (2010) calls the initial program "the strategic brief" and the expanded program "the functional brief".

Initial programming

This initial programming typically consists of the following:

- the rooms and spaces in the building
- approximate total gross floor area of the building

- the number of floors in the building
- approximate budget for the building
- the site

It is important for the client's Project Manager to have some basic programming skills. With this initial program or brief, the client calls a tender to select the consultant team that will design the building. Once the consultants have been selected, the architect (in the consultant team) will continue the programming effort by clarifying and expanding it.

The number and types of rooms and spaces in the building will be decided upon. This will include the floor area, services required and other requirements for each space. The interrelationships between the rooms will be studied and the spaces placed in the most optimal way. Techniques used include adjacency diagrams, stacking diagrams, bubble diagrams.

Circulation between the spaces have to be worked out, both the horizontal and vertical circulation routes. Examples of these are staircases, ramps, lifts and escalators. These circulation routes include fire escape requirements (as part of the Fire Code) and Universal Design requirements that ensure the building is accessible to all.

Once programming is completed, it needs to be signed off by the client so that the architect can move on to the next phase, which is schematic design, where the floor plans are further developed together with the production of elevations and a few sections of the building.

The need for programming

Some designers do design by feel and in a fluid instinctive process while others do design in an orderly, structured plan. Programming provides a structured approach for designers. Pena, one of the leading proponents of architectural programming, in his book **Problem seeking** (2001) said that architectural programming is "A process leading to a statement of an architectural problem and the requirements to be met in offering a solution."

Architectural design is a process of arranging the physical building form to fulfil the desired functions. Architectural programming is a formal structured process where the Owner's need is analysed and provides for a rational basis for design.

The need for programming has grown as buildings have become larger and more complex. Programming fulfils the need for a structured process to plan and organise the various needs of the building occupants and users.

Architects typically do programming as part of their job as they go through the various stages of the design process. However, architectural programming can be a full-time job. There are specialised companies that do programming. The programmer must be able to gather information through various means, have a good understanding of building technology and construction, be familiar with space standards for the building type and compile the information and analysis in the form of a programming report.

There are different levels of programming as owners deal with different sizes of development. This can range from a building like a primary school, to a large mixed-use development like Westgate located in the Jurong Lake District of Singapore, to a mega-project like the Singapore Sports Hub that consists of a stadium, aquatic centre, sports arena and a shopping mall.

There are a number of books that deal with programming or briefing. *Problem seeking – an architectural programming primer* is in its fifth edition and provides an American view of programming. *Architecture in use – an introduction to the programming, design and evaluation of buildings* provides a Dutch viewpoint as it looks at the program of requirements. Finally, *Managing the brief for better design* in its second edition provides a British viewpoint and refers to programming as briefing.

Techniques for information gathering

A lot of information needs to be gathered as part of the programming and site selection processes. There are various techniques that can be used to collect information. These include literature review, interviewing, observation, surveys and workshops.

Literature review involves looking for relevant documents like site reports and construction documents. It could involve searching for laws, regulations, standards, government documents and historical documents. Another useful source of information could be research reports and trade magazines.

A lot of information can be garnered through observation. For example, an inventory of the existing space needs to be carried out. This is done by marking up existing floor plans and taking photos of spaces. Walk-throughs of the building are conducted to observe the level of usage of various spaces and what occupants do in the spaces. Assess the adequacy of these spaces. Observe how occupants move and circulate through the building.

Surveys enable the collection of information from a large number of people. The first step is deciding what information needs to be collected and questions are developed accordingly. Next, a pilot survey can be conducted on a few persons to test the effectiveness of the questions in getting the information required. This is followed by the deployment of the survey to the target respondents and the analysis of the data collected.

Interviewing helps in understanding the goals of the client and what is important to the client organisation in terms of values. Key personnel that need to be interviewed are identified by examining the organisation chart. It is a time-consuming process as there is a need to identify the potential interviewees, contact them and schedule them. To complete the picture, users of the facility and visitors (e.g. customers, partners) to the facility can also be interviewed.

Workshops for stakeholders are useful to discuss the project requirements as a group. In addition to collecting feedback, they are useful for generating ideas and options. Options and requirements can be prioritised at these meetings. In addition to collecting information, the workshops also have the added benefit of building consensus as the participants get to hear from each other and share ideas.

Programming is a team effort. It requires a lot of communication and all the stakeholders need to not just be involved in the process but fully engaged. For the facility manager, it is a golden opportunity to provide input into the renovation or fixing of existing issues in the building(s) and not repeat problems or deficiencies in the existing building(s).

5.2   Essential #5a — Learning the process for programming building spaces

The program can exist in two forms — the initial program (also known as a strategic brief) and a more detailed program (also known as a functional brief).

The initial program is short and outlines the main areas for the architect to look at. This is produced by the Owner's Representative (OwnerRep) or Owner's Project Manager. The purpose of this initial program is to convey to the architect and design team what the intent of the project is, and what the owner would like in his new building. The level of detail of this initial program varies depending on the extent of dedicated manpower available in the Owner's organisation to create it.

After the appointment of the architect, this initial program will be clarified and expanded to become a more detailed program. This will form the basis of the design of the proposed development.

According to Pena (2012), there are five steps in the architectural programming process relating to goals, facts, concepts, needs and a statement of the problem. It moves from the aspirational and ends with the distilled essence of the practical, which is the program of requirements in the form of a report. The five steps are:

1. Determine programming framework and identify project goals
2. Evaluate existing conditions and facts
3. Identify concepts and requirements
4. Determine space requirements
5. Produce programming report

Step 1 – Determine programming framework and identify project goals

In the first step, there is a need to set up the programming framework. It needs to be determined what information needs to be collected and the techniques that will be used for gathering the information.

The key personnel for the project need to be identified so that interviews can be set up with these people. This will help to establish what the project goals are. At a broad level, it needs to be ascertained what the client organisation is trying to accomplish with the project. Some of the broad constraints can also be determined at this stage by asking "When must the project be completed?" and "What is the project budget?"

At this point, stakeholders in the project should be identified in order to involve them at the right time in the programming process.

Step 2 – Evaluate existing conditions and facts

The second step is to evaluate existing conditions (activities, renovate or build new, site) and facts.

In terms of existing conditions, this is done by examining how required activities are being done currently. If there are existing buildings which are similar to the proposed building, they should be examined to see how they are performing. Some questions that need to be asked are:

• How are current activities being carried out?
• Are there existing buildings that can be renovated?
• Or should new buildings be constructed to fulfil the project goals?

In some cases, the site of the new building is fixed before the programming process begins and this site is a constraint that cannot be changed. In other cases, the building program is completed before a site is selected. Yet in others, it is somewhere in between, with the program and site being adjusted in the decision-making process as the constraints are being traded off. If there is a site or a potential site in mind, the existing conditions of the site needs to be examined. This site selection process and evaluation criteria are examined in the later part of this chapter.

The facts that could affect the project need to be identified and evaluated. These facts include the project budget and finances available, the amount of time to complete the building project, etc.

Step 3 – Identify concepts and requirements

The various concepts and requirements that need to be incorporated into the new building needs to be considered and decided upon.

Pena (2012) suggests a list of 24 programmatic concepts that will be further elaborated upon in the next section of the book. This list is useful as a checklist to ensure that no area is missed out when identifying requirements. I have grouped these concepts into the following nine categories:

1. Primary Concepts
2. Urban Planning issues
3. People
4. Activities and Services
5. Types of flow
6. Safety and Security
7. Environmental
8. Construction-related
9. Office-related

Another way to look at this is to consider the requirements and decide which are the requirements that will be the final ones locked into the design. Examples of these include the following:

- User requirements – Identify building requirements with respect to users and activities.
- Future expansion requirements – Allow for future growth and expansion.
- Regulatory requirements – Identify laws and regulations that might impact the building.

- Sustainability requirements – Identify sustainability requirements for the building.
- Relationships and adjacencies – Identify relationships between user groups and room adjacencies (i.e. which rooms need to be near each other). Create zones for each type of use.

Step 4 – Determine space requirements

The fourth step is to determine the space requirements. Based on a list of rooms and spaces, the floor area of each space needs to be determined.

Support areas like mechanical and electrical rooms need to be accounted for. A percentage can also be utilised for the circulation areas at this stage in order to get an estimate of the total floor area of the building.

This information is needed for the architect to lay out the spaces in the design and for the quantity surveyor to estimate the cost of the building.

Step 5 – Produce programming report

The fifth step is to create a programming report. This report will form the basis for the design of the proposed building.

The programming report must contain:

- Project goals – Organisational, Image, Functional, Sustainability, Financial, Time
- Site and Space design criteria – Site analysis, Space inventory, Regulations
- Design performance criteria – Energy usage, Green building standard (e.g. LEED, Green Mark), Systems
- Space relationships and adjacencies (site and building)
- Space requirements (site and building)

Room data sheets are also part of the programming report. It outlines the requirements and needs of each room in the building.

A Room Data Sheet includes:

- Project Title
- Project Description
- Room Name and Function
  - Room name, Function, Area (m²), Number of occupants, Special considerations
- Functional Relationships
  - Room Adjacencies, Floor Adjacencies, Activities
- Material and Finish requirements
  - Floor, Wall, Ceiling, Door, Windows
- Systems Requirements
  - Mechanical systems: Water/Wastewater, Temperature and Humidity, Ventilation
  - Electrical systems: Electrical, Lighting, Communications
  - Special systems
- Miscellaneous Requirements
  - Controls, Access Control, Accessories, Fire extinguishers, Signage/ Wayfinding, Others
- Furniture and Equipment
  - Furniture, Equipment, Floor Plan

Finally, it needs to be remembered that there is a need to balance time, cost, quality and requirements in the process of programming. Once programming is completed, the design process can commence using the building programme as a guide and a check for the final design. The building programme may continue to evolve and be amended as the design process moves forward.

5.3 Programmatic concepts

Pena (2012) suggests a list of 24 programmatic concepts. He defines programmatic concepts as "Abstract ideas intended mainly as functional solutions to client's performance problems without regard to physical responses." In my view, this list is useful as it gives the

OwnerRep or architectural programmer a checklist to think through as the building programme is developed and expanded.

The 24 programmatic concepts can be grouped into nine categories:

Table 5.1   Nine programmatic concept categories.

	Category	Programmatic Concepts (Pena, 2012)
1	Primary Concepts	Priority, Hierarchy, Character
2	Urban Planning issues	Density, Neighbours
3	People	People Grouping, Relationships, Communications
4	Activities and Services	Activity grouping, Service grouping, Accessibility, Orientation, Flexibility, Tolerance
5	Types of flow	Separated Flow, Mixed Flow, Sequential Flow
6	Safety and Security	Safety, Security Controls
7	Environmental	Energy Conservation, Environmental Controls
8	Construction-related	Phasing, Cost Control
9	Office-related	On-premise: Fixed address, Free address Off-premise: Satellite office, Telecommuting, Virtual office

Let us examine the first eight categories of programmatic concepts in the context of hotels. The office-related programmatic concepts will be discussed in the later chapter about office planning and design.

Category 1: Primary concepts (Priority, Hierarchy, Character)

There are three primary concepts to consider: Character, Priority and Hierarchy.

Character is the image the client wants to project in terms of values. What character does your building want to project? In terms of hotel examples, a hotel like the Marina Bay Sands in Singapore with its iconic rooftop infinity pool has the character of being a distinct and unique integrated resort, while the ParkRoyal on Pickering, a hotel with lush greenery and a Green Mark Platinum award, has an image of being a garden hotel.

Priority speaks to the ranking of values in order of importance. There are many different values that are important and that need to be incorporated into a building project. For example in a hotel project, values like sustainability, economy, luxury, and iconic might be the top values for a hotel owner. These need to be ranked and the relative importance of each needs to be decided. The end result would be different if sustainability was placed above economy versus economy above sustainability. In the former, green features that are more costly might still be rolled out, while in the latter the more costly green features might be removed in the light of economic considerations.

Hierarchy refers to people and features in the building that can be placed in order of importance. For example, in a hotel, there can be a hierarchical order to the room sizes. Hotels have different room sizes to meet the varying needs and price points of different guests: e.g. standard room, deluxe room, presidential suites.

Category 2: Urban planning issues (Density, Neighbours)

In the category of urban planning issues, there are two programmatic concepts: Density and Neighbours.

Density refers to the intensity of land use. It can also refer to the density of space use in the building. Is the development low, medium or high density? How dense does the Owner want the development to be? Is the building going to be high rise or low rise? For example, the Marina Bay Sands Hotel has a plot ratio of 3.75 with three 55-storey towers and a large podium.

Neighbours considers the buildings and other features in the vicinity of the development. i.e. Is the building independent or interdependent on their neighbours? For example, the Marina Bay Sands Hotel is interdependent on its neighbours in the same facility, which are tourist attractions like the ArtScience Museum and the Casino. It is also interdependent on its neighbour, Gardens by the Bay, a 100-hectare green space with conservatories and themed gardens, which is linked to the Marina Bay Sands Hotel by an overhead bridge.

Category 3: People (People grouping, Relationships, Communications)

The following programmatic concepts relate to people: People grouping, Relationships, Communications.

People Grouping refers to whether people using the spaces in the facility are individuals, small groups or large groups. In a hotel, the guest rooms will be for individuals, pairs or families. The restaurants will be configured for small groups while the banquet areas will be for large groups. Another consideration will be whether each space is for the exclusive use or shared among various people or groups.

Relationships between people's activities in the facility needs to be considered. The correct interrelation of spaces promotes efficiencies and improves the user experience. In a hotel, the relationships between the lobby, front office, guest rooms, restaurants, kitchen, meeting rooms, parking and administrative offices need to be carefully planned for the hotel building to perform optimally.

Communications is a programmatic concept relating to the networks and patterns of communication. How do people communicate with each other in the hotel? What communication networks need to be put in place in the hotel? Guest room communications, hotel staff communications, convention and meeting communications are examples of concepts that need to be decided upon during the programming phase.

Category 4: Activities and Services (Activity grouping, Service grouping, Accessibility, Orientation, Flexibility, Tolerance)

Are there things to be grouped? These could be grouped for reasons of efficiency and convenience. There are two concepts that deal with grouping: Activity grouping and Service grouping.

Activity grouping considers activities that occur in the facility. Are the various activities going to be integrated or compartmentalised with separate zones for each activity? Using a hotel example, there could be separate zones for guest rooms, recreational areas and restaurants. Alternatively, these could be all integrated and all mixed together without clearly defined zones.

Service grouping considers services in the facility. Are they centralised or decentralised? For example, is the hotel kitchen centralised? Is there one central kitchen or multiple kitchens for the various restaurants? With one central kitchen, there could be a potential savings in manpower and sharing of kitchen equipment. However, there might be an increase in walking distance for waiters if there is only one kitchen for several restaurants.

In terms of movement and wayfinding, there are two concepts: Accessibility and Orientation.

Accessibility looks at the provisions for people with disabilities, visitor wayfinding and transport connections. There are two aspects to accessibility. The first is internal accessibility in terms of handicap accessibility and wayfinding and signage. For example, the Marina Bay Sands development is a very large development so there needs to be adequate signage for visitors and guests to find their way around the building. In addition to conforming to handicap accessibility requirements, the development also has a wheelchair loan service. The second is in terms of transport connections, it is adequately linked to public transport with connections to the Bayfront MRT[1] station as well as bus stops. There are also good road connections with two major expressways nearby.

Orientation considers how the users find their way around within a building or campus in regard to wayfinding. Having unique features like a sculpture or water feature helps to providing a point of reference for guests in a large hotel to orientate themselves when moving from one part of the hotel to another.

The concepts of Flexibility and Tolerance go hand in hand.

Flexibility considers the ability for the facility to be expanded, converted to other uses and whether it can be used for various uses. An example is the hotel's meeting spaces where there needs to be flexibility to accommodate different types of meetings so the number and size of the meetings spaces must be planned so that it is able to be converted to suit the varying needs of guests.

Tolerance looks at the tightness of fit for activities for a particular space. Is it precisely the size needed for the function? Or is there additional space catered for expansion or additional activity? Using the same hotel example, are the meeting rooms sized precisely for a fixed number of persons with no room for increase or is it a loose fit to allow for a small percentage of increase in the number of persons that can be accommodated?

Category 5: Types of flow (Separated Flow, Mixed Flow, Sequential Flow)

There are three types of flow to need to be considered: Separated Flow, Mixed Flow, Sequential Flow.

---

[1] Mass Rapid Transit (MRT). Singapore's rapid transit railway system.

Separated Flow is when the various streams of circulation have their own exclusive channels with minimal crossings. For safety and convenience, the flow of pedestrians and vehicles are typically separated as far as possible. In a resort hotel setting where the hotel is spread out over a large area, care needs to be taken to keep the flow of hotel guests separate from the flow of vehicles as far as possible to ensure safety and to create a pleasant ambience for guests.

Mixed Flow is when the various circulation patterns intermingle. The hotel lobby is a multi-purpose area to link the guest rooms, restaurants, amenities and function areas. Hence there is a mixed flow in that area and there is multi-directional flow of people. The lobby needs to be adequately sized and special care needs to be taken to ensure easy wayfinding.

Sequential Flow occurs when people or things progress in a sequence of steps through the facility. Examples of this type of flow include the progression of people in an airport terminal and the progression of things in a factory. In a hotel, there is a sequential flow of the hotel guest from the drop-off point to the lobby reception area to the guest room.

Category 6: Safety and Security (Safety, Security)

Safety in building programming relates to life safety, building codes and safety precautions. One key aspect of safety is to ensure the safety of the building's occupants. Fire protection in the form of alarms and sprinklers are an important aspect of ensuring the safety of guests, users and staff of a hotel.

Security ensures that access to the property is limited to authorised persons. It also helps to protect the occupants and the property. The degree of security control (minimum, medium, maximum) for the different areas need to decided. For example, access to guest rooms and floors needs to be controlled for privacy and to deter crime. Many hotels these days use key cards to control access to guest rooms.

Category 7: Environmental (Energy Conservation, Environmental Control)

Two of the programmatic concepts relate to environmental issues: Energy Conservation and Environmental Control.

Energy Conservation examines how to reduce or minimise energy usage in the facility. In tropical climates, cooling the building accounts for the largest use of energy in a building. Keeping cooled areas to a minimum will greatly help in this effort. In temperate climates, the focus will be on heating. Another area for energy conservation is lighting. Hotels can be designed in a way to allow for natural daylight to enter and thus reduce the need for artificial lighting.

Environmental Control considers how the facility's environment can be managed for people's comfort. This is done by controlling the air temperature, light and sound. The areas that need to be looked at include both the areas within the building envelope and outside it. Resort hotels have naturally ventilated corridors sheltered by greenery to provide a pleasant environment for their guests as well as conserve energy by reducing the need for cooling.

Category 8: Construction-related (Phasing, Cost Control)

The construction-related programmatic concepts are Phasing and Cost Control.

Phasing considers whether the development will be constructed and completed in one stage or in a few stages. The questions asked are "Will there be phasing of construction?" and "Is there an urgent need to occupy the building that will lead to the earlier completion of more critical portions of the building?" For example, in a large resort development, the project can be planned in a few phases to manage the financial risk of having one large investment.

Cost Control looks at how to manage the cost of a facility. It looks at ideas that will lead to the completion of the building project within the available funds. For hotels, this could be adjusting the level of finish, reducing the number of high-cost items like water features, or reducing the size of the development.

5.4 Essential #5b – Site selection process

The programming of the building and selection of the site go hand in hand. Even though they are considered as separate processes, they do not exist exclusively; each process affects the other.

Which comes first? The building program or the site? Many owners determine the building program first and then select a site that can accommodate it. The completion of the building program clarifies user needs and space requirements. In some cases, owners decide on the site first and then develop a building program that can fit on the site. Yet others will develop the building program and site concurrently.

Steps in the site selection process

Let us consider the situation where the building program is first drawn up and then a site is selected. The following are the steps for site selection process:

1. Program investigation
2. Shortlist of potential sites
3. Site inventory and analysis
4. Site evaluation
5. Develop report and present for approval

The first step is **program investigation**. Based on the program, the building footprint, area required for parking, circulation, external areas are extracted to determine the size of site required. This provides the minimum size of the building site required.

The second step is to draw up a **shortlist of potential sites** based on the minimum size required, required adjacencies and availability of the sites.

The third step is to **take inventory and analyse the various characteristics of each site**. The physical (e.g. topography, geotechnical conditions, utilities), cultural (e.g. existing land use, ownership), and regulatory (e.g. zoning requirements, environmental regulations) characteristics of a site are explored. The depth of the analysis will depend on the owner, the size and complexity of the project size and the actual site being analysed.

The fourth step is to **evaluate the sites** by comparing them. The total scores of the various sites are compared to determine the most appropriate site. This is compared against a list of evaluation criteria. Each criterion would have varying weightages to reflect its relative importance. This is typically done by a committee that represents the various interests in the project.

The last step is to formalise the decision and document the decision-making process by compiling a **report**. A presentation is made to the approving parties and a final site selection is made.

5.5 Site evaluation criteria

This section expands on the criteria for evaluating potential sites for development. As mentioned in the earlier section, evaluation criteria need to be set out. Weightage need to be assigned to each criterion to reflect the level of importance of each criterion. The criteria used, and their assigned weightage varies, and need to be decided upon based on the specific needs of the development.

A possible list of criteria that can be used is as follows:

- Accommodate the building program
- Physical characteristics of the site
- Accessibility of the site
- Availability of utilities
- Cost
- Compatibility with neighbouring uses
- Availability for use
- Potential for expansion

Let us consider the criteria using an example of a new building being constructed for the Faculty of Built Environment on a university campus. The new building will accommodate new studios, maker spaces, labs, classrooms, student areas and faculty offices.

The first criterion that needs to be considered is how well the **building program** can be accommodated on the site. The site must be able to accommodate the building program of requirements which includes the minimum gross floor area mentioned before. If there are planning and zoning regulations, these need to be studied and checked to ensure compliance. Examples of these regulations include land use, setback, plot ratio, etc.

The second criterion is the **physical characteristics** of the site. For example, the topography of the site. Is the site flat or sloping? The geotechnical conditions of the site need to be considered. How are the soil conditions of the site? What type of foundations are needed to support the building? The presence of trees and water features on site are another consideration. Are there trees that need to be relocated? Can the streams be built over?

The third criterion is the **accessibility** of the site. Is the site adjacent to the other faculty buildings? Are students able to access the building easily? Are there transport connections like roads and public transport? How far is the nearest bus stop? Is there a service road for the delivery of goods? Is there a drop-off point for visitors to the building?

The fourth criterion is the **availability of utilities** at the site. Examples of utilities are water, electricity, sewerage (wastewater), and telecommunication connections. Is there enough capacity in the utilities to service this new building? Having to construct new or additional utility connections could add time and cost to the project.

The fifth criterion is **cost**. How much does the site cost? How much does it cost to develop the site including the cost of the building and infrastructure? For the university, the site is typically on the campus that it already owns, so the cost is primarily for the construction of the building. However, many universities are public institutions and are accountable for public funds, so cost is an important criterion.

The sixth criterion is **compatibility to neighbouring uses**. Will the neighbours be adversely affected by this building? Is there synergy in terms of the new building's use with the neighbouring buildings? For example, the new building should be near the other faculty buildings so that students and staff can move easily between faculty buildings.

The seventh criterion is **availability**. Is the land available for use? Does the university own the land? Does the land need to be cleared? Are there easements granted that prevent the use of the site for a building? Are there underground services that need to be relocated before the site can be used? If there are large underground services like large electrical cables or plumbing that need to be diverted, the time taken to do this might be too long or the cost might be so prohibitive that another site would be considered.

The eighth criterion is the **potential for expansion**. Can this building be easily expanded in the future? When the faculty needs to expand again, is there space for another building to be built near this new building? This is an important consideration as many universities have limited land, and take a long-term view of development. They will have to live with their construction decisions many years down the road. It is therefore important to think long-term for buildings on a university campus.

Site evaluation form

The factors, weightage and the score for each site to be considered can be tabulated in a form shown in Table 5.2. The site with the highest score will be the most suitable site for the development.

Table 5.2   Example of site evaluation form.

Project Name:							
Site Evaluation Committee (Names):							
	Factors	Weightage	Site A	Site B	Site C	Site D	Site E
1	Location						
2	Size and shape of site						
3	Physical Characteristics						
4	Utilities						
5	Parking						
6	Accessibility						
7	Ability to expand						
8	Cost						
9	Availability						
	Total Score						
Other comments:							

References

Blyth, A., & Worthington, J. (2010). *Managing the brief for better design.* Routledge.

California Department of Education website (2018), "School site selection and approval guide", available at: https://www.cde.ca.gov/ls/fa/sf/schoolsiteguide.asp (accessed 12 Jul 2018)

Demkin, J. A. (2001). *The architect's handbook of professional practice* (Vol. 1). John Wiley & Sons.

Iowa State University (2018), "Planning, Design, and Construction", available at: https://www.fpm.iastate.edu/planning/ (accessed 12 Jul 2018)

LaGro Jr, J. A. (2011). *Site analysis: A contextual approach to sustainable land planning and site design*. John Wiley & Sons.

Pena, W. M., & Parshall, S. A. (2012). *Problem seeking: An architectural programming primer*. John Wiley & Sons.

Preiser, W., & Vischer, J. (Eds.). (2006). *Assessing building performance*. Routledge.

University of Illinois (2003), "Site Selection Process", available at: http://fs.illinois.edu/docs/default-source/capital-programs/site-selection-process.pdf?sfvrsn=0 (accessed 12 Jul 2018)

van der Voordt, D. J. M., & Wegen, H. B. (2005). *Architecture in use: an introduction to the programming, design and evaluation of buildings*. Routledge.

PART 2

Campus Planning and Design

CHAPTER 6

Facility Master Planning

In this chapter, you will learn about the following:

1. Urban planning
2. The facility master plan
3. Essential #6 – Learning about the master planning process
4. Case study: Airport master plan
5. Case study: University master plan

Essential #6

Learn about the master planning process so that the long-term phased development of a facility's campus is optimised.

In the earlier chapters, we have been examining planning and design at the building scale. In this and the next chapter, we will be exploring planning and design at a campus scale.

In this chapter, we will be exploring the process of master planning at a campus scale in the context of two types of large-scale developments: an airport and a university. An airport campus will be in the range of thousands of hectares while a large university is in the range of hundreds of hectares. For example, Singapore Changi Airport is currently about 1700 hectares in size while the National University of Singapore has a campus of about 200 hectares.

6.1 Urban planning

Before exploring the process of master planning, there is a need to understand the urban context in which the campus is situated in. This is achieved by understanding urban planning and urban plans because this is the context in which our facility master plan and facilities are situated in. In this book, the term "urban planning" will be used rather than the British term "town planning".

There are different types of plans related to urban planning. Table 6.1 lists a few types of urban plans with accompanying Singaporean examples and the government agencies responsible for them (in parentheses). Readers can refer to planning publications produced by planning associations like the American Planning Association to get an in-depth description of each type of urban plan or refer to the websites of the various government agencies to see examples of each type of urban plan.

Table 6.1   Types of urban plans and examples of them.

	Type of Urban Plan	Examples from Singapore
1	Comprehensive plan	Master Plan (Urban Redevelopment Authority)
2	Neighbourhood plan	Jurong Lake District Plan (Urban Redevelopment Authority), Toa Payoh Town Plan (Housing Development Board), Punggol Town Plan (Housing Development Board)
3	Transportation plan	Land Transport Plan (Land Transport Authority), Cycling Plan (Land Transport Authority)
4	Park plan	Park Connector Plan, East Coast Regional Park Plan, Sembawang Regional Park Plan (National Parks Board)
5	Housing plan	Housing Plan (Housing Development Board)

Many cities have a planning authority that is responsible for regulating land use in the city. The extent of regulation varies from city to city.

The Urban Redevelopment Authority (URA), the Singapore government authority responsible for land use, is responsible for the urban planning of Singapore. There are two key plans that the URA uses to guide land-use in Singapore: The Concept Plan and the Master Plan.

The **Concept Plan** is the long-term land-use plan for the strategic development of Singapore with a focus on accommodating a growing population and supporting economic growth. The time horizon for this plan is 40 to 50 years and is reviewed every ten years. The plan has zones for various land-uses including residential, commercial, industry, recreation, infrastructure, institution, special use, and reserve use. The water bodies, like reservoirs and rivers, are also marked out on the concept plan. Transportation networks like roads and rail are also indicated on the plan.

The **Master Plan** which translates the Concept Plan into a more detailed implementation plan that has a 10 to 15-year outlook. This statutory document is revised every five years. It guides the development of land through the regulation of land-use and density. The plan is both comprehensive and integrated. Social, economic and environmental aspects are considered and there is consultation with other government bodies and the public.

In addition to the Master Plan for entire city-state of Singapore, there are also master plans for specific areas. These include the Jurong Lake District (360 hectares), Woodlands Regional Centre (more than 100 hectares), and Punggol Digital District (50 hectares).

For example, the Jurong Lake District Master Plan covers a 360 hectare area that includes the Jurong gateway around the existing Jurong East MRT station, the Lakeside gateway which is expected to house the future station for the High Speed Rail between Singapore and Kuala Lumpur, and the Jurong Lake Gardens where the existing Chinese and Japanese Gardens are situated. The Jurong Lake District will be mixed-use with different land uses ranging from commercial to residential to recreational.

Closely associated to Urban Planning is Urban Design. Like urban planning, urban design deals with land use and the shaping of the urban landscape. The difference is in the focus, with urban planning being more technical in nature while urban design is more artistic and aesthetic in focus.

6.2 The facility master plan – Planning on a campus level

Having considered the urban and city planning framework in which the facility is situated in, we will now look at what a facility master plan is, the components of a master plan, the stakeholders in a master plan, and examples of facility master plans.

What is a facility master plan?

There are various terms used for this including master plan, facility master plan and campus master plan. According to the International Facility Management Association's (IFMA) Strategic facility planning paper, a master plan is the "Site-specific integration of programmed elements, natural conditions and constructed infrastructure and systems at the functional, aesthetic and temporal (time) levels."

The facility master plan guides the long-term development for a site. Since these sites are typically very large, a lot of the buildings and facilities will be built over an extended time-period. Hence the typical time horizon for such a plan is 15 to 20 years.

The master plan must address the needs of the users and occupants of the site. It will have to account for natural conditions like topography and waterways. The plan will influence surrounding neighbours as much as it will be influenced by them; for example, through pollution and socio-economic impacts.

Transportation connections also needs to be addressed. For example, for Bidadari New Town, its master plan must consider how town residents going to get to other parts of Singapore.

Community engagement is also part of the master planning process — not just to address technical concerns, but also to listen to the concerns of the neighbours especially in regard to the negative impacts of a project, e.g., noise issues from airports.

What are the components of a facility master plan?

There are four components of a facility master plan. These are the programmed elements, regulatory requirements, time and cost.

A master plan is created in response to program requirements. Each master plan will have **elements** to fulfil specific parts of the program. For example, in an airport, the programmed elements will be the runways, taxiways, aircraft parking aprons, terminal building, parking and roadway access. For a university campus, the programmed elements will be educational spaces, research spaces, administrative spaces, walking paths, parking, and the roadway system.

The master plan will have to respond to **regulatory requirements**. As mentioned earlier, most cities have a master plan (comprehensive plan) that guides development. This is done through zoning laws that regulate the type of land use and density of development. The facility master plan must consider these laws as well as how to connect to the surrounding urban fabric.

In terms of **time**, the phasing element needs to be studied carefully. The master plan will have a campus plan showing the existing buildings and proposed buildings. The proposed buildings will have to be phased to show which buildings are needed in the short-term and which buildings are needed in the longer term. Having this distinction allows for the planning of the campus to take a long-term view but yet be relevant for the short-term as it shows the buildings that will need to be constructed over the next few years. For master plans with a 20-year time horizon, there could be three phases: the short-term phase (5 years), medium-term phase (10 years) and long-term (20 years).

The fourth component of a master plan that has to be considered is **costs**. Development of a campus is costly and getting the financial resources to fund buildings takes time. Having the cost estimate for each phase of development is useful information to furnish to the decision-makers, stakeholders and financial staff for them to raise or allocate the financial resources necessary. For example, a state university that has a growing student population will need to build more facilities, and having an estimate of the cost of the buildings needed in the next few years will allow money to be sought by issuing bonds, getting grants or by fund-raising.

Stakeholders – Government

When putting together a master plan, there are many government agencies that will be involved in the plan. There is a need to get all the government agencies involved because they are the key stakeholders in the development of a large facility. Many large facilities with campuses are government-related. Examples of these are universities, airports, and hospitals.

In Singapore, an understanding of this is even more critical as the government is the owner of a large portion of the land through its various agencies. For example, in order to develop a new airport in Singapore, the airport operator will have to interact with the following government agencies:

Table 6.2   Examples of government agencies involved in the building of an airport in Singapore.

	Government Agency (in Singapore)	Description
1	Ministry of Transport (MOT)	Has jurisdiction and oversight over air transport matters.
	Civil Aviation Authority of Singapore (CAAS), a statutory board under MOT	Responsible for air transport matters in Singapore. Responsible for air traffic control and air transport regulatory matters including airport regulation.
	Land Transport Authority (LTA), a statutory board under MOT	Responsible for land transport matters including land transport connections to airport; e.g. expressways, rail, bus.

(Continued)

Table 6.2   (*Continued*)

	Government Agency (in Singapore)	Description
2	Ministry of Finance	Deals with national finances including funding of the new airport.
3	Ministry of Environment and Water Resources (MEWR)	Manages the national environment ensuring a quality living environment. Ensures that the airport has good drainage infrastructure to prevent flooding.
4	Ministry of Law (MinLaw)	Manages national legal issues.
	Singapore Land Authority (SLA), a statutory board under MinLaw	Deals with land issues for the new airport.
5	Ministry of National Development (MND)	Oversees national development and infrastructure.
	Urban Redevelopment Authority (URA), a statutory board under MND	Regulates land use and zoning issues. Ensures that the new airport is in a location that is compatible with neighbouring land uses.
	Building and Construction Authority (BCA), a statutory board under MND	Responsible for building and construction related matters. Ensures that the airport buildings are safe for occupation.
6	Ministry of Home Affairs (MHA)	Responsible for security issues including airport security issues.

*list is not exhaustive and is meant to highlight some of the main agencies that need to be dealt with.

Examples of facility master plans

Many of the larger facilities have a large land area, so there is a need for a campus level master plan to guide the orderly development of the property. Examples of large facilities in Singapore that would have master plans on the campus level are listed in Table 6.3.

To illustrate the large size of some of the facilities, the area they occupy are given in the brackets.

Table 6.3   Examples of large facilities in Singapore with campus level master plans.

	Facility Type	Examples of Singapore Facilities with Master Plans
1	Airport	Changi Airport (approx. 2600 ha)
2	Seaport	Tuas Port, Pasir Panjang Port
3	Leisure	Sentosa, Mandai Nature Park
4	Garden	Singapore Botanic Gardens
5	Educational	National University of Singapore (approx. 200 ha), Nanyang Technological University, Singapore Institute of Technology
6	Industrial	One-North, Cleantech Park
7	Military	Changi Airbase
8	Healthcare	Health City Novena (approx. 20 ha), Singapore General Hospital (approx. 50 ha)
9	Housing	Bidadari New Town, Tengah New Town

6.3   Essential #6 – Learning about the master planning process

There are 6 steps in the master planning process. These are:

1. Inventory
2. Forecasts
3. Facility requirements
4. Alternative concepts
5. Preferred development plan
6. Implementation plan

Step 1 – Inventory

At the Inventory step, a list of the existing facilities on site is collated. Depending on the type of facility, this can be in terms of land area (in hectares) or in terms of floor area (square metres) or in terms of a count (number). Often times, this is a combination of land area, floor area and a count.

For example, in a plan for a township, there will be different uses of land. The inventory will contain a breakdown of land use by type of land-use, e.g. residential, commercial, recreational, institutional, and community. This will be expressed in hectares.

Another way is to measure the gross floor area of all the buildings and report it in terms of square metres. An example of this will be for a university campus, this will be reported in the following categories: teaching, research, and support.

The inventory can also be expressed in terms of a number. This is particularly useful for spaces built to standard sizes, such as parking spaces for vehicles, which many facilities have. For example, this can be itemised or recorded as '4500 parking spaces' on the inventory.

Step 2 – Forecasts

In the second step, forecasts estimating the demand expected must be made.

Given that a master plan is a long-term facility plan, the forecast is typically a long-term one, reviewed annually, and done up to 15 to 30 years out. What is forecasted is dependent on the type of facility, the users and types of activities accommodated. For example, for an airport, a forecast of passengers, cargo and aircraft operations will need to be made.

Step 3 – Facility requirements

The next step will be to calculate and put together facility requirements based on the forecast. A common way to do this is to compile these requirements for a few points of this forecast. A typical master plan would have facility requirements corresponding with the three periods:

- Short-term: 5 years
- Medium-term: 10 years
- Long-term: 20 years

Step 4 – Alternative concepts

Alternative concepts are developed based on the requirements. There is more than one way that the facility requirements can be fulfilled on the campus of a facility. The planner will put together several schemes, each of them having varying levels of advantages and disadvantages in different areas. To integrate all the views and concerns of stakeholders, a scoring matrix of the various concepts and weighted factors is drawn up. This will allow a final concept to be selected.

Step 5 – Preferred development plan

A preferred development plan is developed next. This helps to flesh out the selected scheme to a level where all the key details are incorporated. In jurisdictions where environmental concerns are paramount, this plan will have to undergo a detailed environmental assessment, to ensure that environmental impacts are minimised or mitigated.

Step 6 – Implementation plan

The final step in the master planning process is the implementation plan. This will include the phasing of the development and the cost of each phase of the development. To allow the development to be carried out in a phased manner according to the needs and financial ability of the facility's stakeholders, the plan may also include a section that identifies funding sources.

Master plans are always subject to change. For example, in a university, an area set aside for the future expansion of student housing could be repurposed for the construction of a new academic building to support a new and emerging field.

Master plans are reviewed every five to ten years either as a requirement imposed by a regulatory authority or when the current master plan is obsolete as a result of changes in the operating environment.

6.4 Case study: Airport master plan

Let us consider an airport master plan. An airport has many technical requirements with a high emphasis on safety and security. These technical requirements, particularly for the airside portion of the airport, ensure that aircraft can operate safely. These technical requirements tend to take a primary role in the design considerations. The focus of airports is to allow passengers and cargo to depart and arrive safely and efficiently.

Purpose and goals of the master plan

There is always a purpose for the master plan study. For example, is the master plan for a new airport or an existing airport? Is this a revision of an older master plan that the airport had done 10 years ago?

What goals are you trying to achieve? Typical goals for an airport master plan include:

- Catering for future growth
- Involving all stakeholders in a structured way
- Improving the passenger experience
- Phasing development based on need and finance available
- Ensuring safe and efficient air transportation for the community
- Minimising the environmental impact of the development

Airport master planning process

Using the framework previously established in the last section, let us look at the airport master planning process. A typical airport master plan report will take between one to two years to complete.

1. Inventory

The first step is to inventory the various facilities that exist at the airport. For an airport, the this can be divided into airside, terminal, landside and support facilities. Table 6.4 gives examples of facilities found at a typical airport. The inventory will include a description of each type of facility, its current state, and might include a count, the area it occupies and the gross floor area of the building. Dimensions of the facility and its properties are also noted.

Table 6.4   Examples of facilities at a typical airport.

	Categories	Facilities
1	Airside	Runways, Taxiways, Aircraft parking stands
2	Terminal	Check-in hall, Security screening, Gate lounge, Baggage claim, Passport control, Curb (drop off and pick up)
3	Landside	Parking, Roads, Public transport
4	Support	Fuel farm, Cargo, Maintenance hangars

2. Forecasts

Based on various factors (e.g. projected economic growth of the region), a long-term forecast is created for the number of passengers, amount of cargo and number of aircraft movements at the airport. This forecast drives the various facility requirements.

A typical airport master plan will have a 20-year forecast. In addition, optimistic and pessimistic forecasts can be created to create different scenarios.

Table 6.5   List of factors considered in a forecast list for an airport master plan.

	Forecast Item	Affects the Following Facility Requirements
1	Passengers (number)	Passenger Terminal facilities, Parking
2	Cargo (tons)	Cargo facilities
3	Aircraft movements	Runways, Taxiways, Aircraft parking stands

3. Facility requirements

From the forecasts, activity levels for the short-term (5 years), medium-term (10 years) and long-term (20 year) are selected. This allows the short-term, medium-term and long-term facility requirements to be calculated. This will be expressed in various ways. For example, terminal building requirements will be in square metres, while aircraft parking stands will be forecasted in terms of the number needed.

4. Alternative concepts

Based on the facility requirements, various possibilities for each element is created. After a screening process of various possibilities, the next step is to bring together the various elements and integrate them in various combinations. Then a final screening of each combination conducted, to pick the most appropriate one.

An example would be alternatives in various series — which we shall refer to as A series (A1 to A7), and B series (B1 to B3). In each of the series, the passenger terminal is in a different location. Each alternative is basically a different combination of different patterns of the airside, terminal, landside and support elements.

In order to whittle the long list of alternatives to two or three final options, a list of evaluation criteria with a weighting factor is used. Through a workshop process, one of the layout options is finally chosen. The reasons for this choice are then documented in the Master Plan report for future reference.

For countries with extensive environmental regulations, an environmental screening of the preferred development alternative will have to be performed.

5. Preferred development plan

The preferred development plan is typically divided into 3 phases: short-term, medium-term and long-term. An example of this could be 5 years, 10 years and 20 years.

Likewise, the cost of the development needs to be estimated and split into phases corresponding to the time span(s) chosen.

6. Implementation plan

The next step is to decide what portions of the preferred development plan needs to be executed immediately. This generally corresponds with short-term portion of the preferred development plan. This needs to be put on the airport's capital plan. As part of the capital plan, sources of financing need to be secured for the development projects. This will be further elaborated in a later chapter on capital planning.

Given that the forecast is a guess of the activity level in the future, trigger points for each new phase have to be set. To do this, the time taken to develop each type of facility needs to be examined. For example, at an airport in a developed country that has many environmental regulations and extensive public consultation, a reasonable estimate of the time it takes to plan, design and construct a new runway is 15 years.

In regard to expanding a facility like an airport, there are two schools of thought — build ahead of demand or build after there is proven demand. On one hand, building ahead of demand will ensure that there will always be sufficient capacity to cope with rising demands. The flip side of this is: what if the forecasted demand does not happen?

An example of building ahead of demand is Singapore's Changi Airport, that has made the strategic decision to build ahead of demand for two reasons: (1) it is the air hub for the country, and (2) to maintain high service levels and standards.

6.5 Case study: University master plan

Let us now consider master planning in the context of a university campus.

Purpose and goals of the master plan

Large universities have a significant amount of land. Many of them are public universities that have to be good stewards and that need to be accountable to the government and the public for the use of their resources.

As mentioned earlier in the strategic planning chapter, the facility master plan is done in support of the organisation's strategic plan. The master plan often follows the creation of the University Strategic Plan. The following are examples of goals that the university might want to achieve under the facility master plan:

- Allow for expansion
- Rejuvenate an old campus
- Make the campus more sustainable
- Improve the transportation network on campus
- Improve the mobility on campus for pedestrians and cyclists, and users of personal mobility devices (PMDs)
- Improve accessibility
- Improve the student experience
- Integrate the live-study-play student experience

University master planning process

Using the framework previously established in Section 6.3, let us look at the university master planning process.

1. Inventory

The first step is to inventory the various facilities that exist at the university. For a university, this can be divided into academic spaces, research spaces, residential spaces, sports and recreation spaces, and support spaces. Table 6.6 gives examples of facilities found at a typical university.

The inventory will include a description of each building, its current state, the type of spaces it has, the area it occupies and the gross floor area of the building.

Table 6.6   Examples of facilities found at a typical university.

	Categories	Spaces
1	Academic	Lecture theatres, Seminar rooms, Tutorial rooms, Computer rooms
2	Research	Research Labs, Research centres, Research offices
3	Residential	Student housing, Dining halls,
4	Sports and Recreation	Sports facilities, Stadiums, Swimming pools
5	Support	Administrative offices, Maintenance facilities

2. Forecasts and projected needs

Based on the strategic plan and objectives of the university, forecasts and projected needs are worked out. The main drivers for new development on campus is in response to a growth in academic programmes, research programmes or new initiatives by the university.

For example, an increased enrolment in academic programmes would mean the need for more academic spaces for conducting classes. The launch of a new undergraduate programme in a new field might require more teaching spaces or specialised teaching spaces.

In terms of research programmes, the increase in research activities would generate the need for more research labs and offices. The launch of a new area of research might require the construction of new specialised labs to support the new research thrust.

New initiatives by the university could include the increase in the number of students having a residential experience on campus. This would result in the need for more student housing to be planned, designed and built on campus. The new initiative could be also be services-related; for example, to improve the Information Technology (IT) infrastructure on campus. This would involve the construction of enhanced IT infrastructure like laying a new IT network, new IT hub buildings and the related IT rooms throughout the campus.

Examples of metrics used for forecast and projected needs could be the number of undergraduate students, graduate students, academic staff, and administrative staff.

3. Facility requirements

The forecasts and projected needs will next be translated into facility requirements. At a broad level, this will be in terms of number or floor area. For example, the number of rooms required for student housing, the number of lecture theatres, the number of classrooms, the floor area for teaching spaces, etc.

This list of projected facilities will be tabulated. The element of time also needs to be considered. For example, which facilities will need to be built in the next ten years and which facilities need to be built beyond the ten-year period.

4. Alternative concepts

Based on the facility requirements, initial sizing and massing of the buildings will be done. This will be translated into a building footprint that can be placed on the campus plan. For large campuses, the site is divided into smaller portions and laid out in zones or areas.

When compared to the airport master plan described earlier, the university master plan follows more traditional urban planning formats with a focus on the creation of a framework for the campus defined by districts, streets and corridors. The design character and the density of the university campus will be considered. Various building typologies will be examined. Other considerations are the site's topography, transportation links, accessibility, environmental considerations, and future expansion.

Through workshops, feedback is collected on the initial draft plans. Issues raised will be addressed and the draft master plan adjusted.

5. Preferred development plan

Once the best options have been chosen, the final campus plan is compiled. For completeness, the timeline and cost for development is also included in the master plan. This is presented to the university board for approval.

6. Implementation plan

A decision needs to sequence the buildings in the order in which they are to be built. The portions of the campus master plan that need to be built in the short-term needs to be translated into the University's capital improvement plan. For larger campuses, detailed programming for each district will be carried out.

References

American Planning Association. (2006). *Planning and urban design standards*. John Wiley & Sons.
Austin-Bergstrom International Airport (2003), "Airport Master Plan", available at: http://www.austintexas.gov/page/airport-master-plan (accessed 12 Jul 2018)
Channel News Asia (2016), "URA calls for master plan proposals for Singapore's 'second' CBD', the Jurong Lake District", available at: http://www.channelnewsasia.com/news/singapore/ura-calls-for-master-plan/2947206.html (accessed 12 Jul 2018)
International Facility Management Association (2009), "Strategic Facility Planning: A White Paper on Strategic Facility Planning", available at: https://community.ifma.org/cfs-file/__key/telligent-evolution-components-attachments/13-463-00-00-01-05-69-96/2009_5F00_Strategic-Facility-Planning_5F00_White-Paper.pdf (accessed 12 Jul 2018)
Ministry of Communications and Information (2018), "Singapore Government Directory", available at: https://www.gov.sg/sgdi/ministries/ (accessed 10 Aug 2018)
Nanyang Technological University (1995), *Master Plan Report: Nanyang Technological University*, Singapore.
National University of Singapore Campus Infrastructure (2018), "General University Design Guidelines for Kent Ridge Campus", available at: http://www.nus.edu.sg/uci/PPM/DesignGuidelines.htm (accessed 12 Jul 2018)

National University of Singapore Campus Infrastructure (2018), "Third Master Plan", available at: http://www.nus.edu.sg/uci/PPM/ThirdMasterPlan.htm (accessed 12 Jul 2018)

Steiner, F. R. (2018). *Making Plans: How to Engage with Landscape, Design, and the Urban Environment*. University of Texas Press.

The University of Texas at Austin (2018), "Campus Master Plan", available at: http://campusplanning.utexas.edu/masterplan/ (accessed 12 Jul 2018)

The University of Texas System Office of Facilities Planning and Construction (2011), "Campus Master Planning Guidelines", available at: https://www.utsystem.edu/sites/default/files/offices/facilities-planning-construction/CampusMasterPlan/20111201_Update_UT%20System_OFPC_CMP_Guidelines.pdf (accessed 12 Jul 2018)

Urban Redevelopment Authority (2018), "Planning", available at: https://www.ura.gov.sg/Corporate/Planning (accessed 17 Mar 2018)

Urban Redevelopment Authority (2018), "Jurong Lake District – A lakeside destination for business and leisure", available at: https://www.ura.gov.sg/sales/BLWay/JLD-brochure.pdf (accessed 12 Jul 2018)

CHAPTER 7

Environmental Planning

In this chapter, you will learn about the following:

1. Essential #7a – Understanding the environmental impacts of development

2. Essential #7b – Learning the key aspects of the environmental impact assessment process

3. Stakeholders

4. Case study: Hong Kong International Airport Three Runway System

Essential #7

Understand the environmental impacts of development and learn the key aspects of the environmental impact assessment process.

Environmental planning is a specialised area of planning that accompanies large-scale projects. It is an extension of master planning particularly when it is the first master plan being done for a large site or when the master plan is expanded to cover a large new area that was not included in an older master plan.

Large developments impact the environment in many ways. The various aspects of environmental impact are explored in the first part of this chapter. There is a need for legislation that ensures that the environment is protected from adverse effects. Environmental legislation is examined at the start of environmental planning so that the planned development is compliant.

In many countries, there is legislation that requires an Environmental Impact Assessment (EIA) to be carried out for large-scale developments. This chapter reviews the various steps in the EIA process, which include scoping the project, exploring various alternatives, and examining the environmental impacts and mitigation measures. The importance of stakeholder engagement is also emphasised as it is the heart of the EIA process.

The chapter closes with a case study of the Hong Kong International Airport Three Runway System.

7.1   Essential #7a – Understanding the environmental impacts of development

There are various forms of environmental impact that are the result of large developments. Air quality is one aspect that needs to be examined as air quality might be affected because of emissions by construction vehicles and dust from construction vehicles and construction activities. Developments also impact water resources on the site(s), sometimes to the extent of polluting lakes, streams the sea, etc.

Clearing land to establish a development site also impacts biodiversity as there is a loss of habitat for plants and animals. Then there is also noise pollution that often arises from construction activities, which will affect surrounding areas. There might also be a loss of historical or cultural heritage as a result of the disturbance or destruction of historical or cultural artefacts during any phase of development. The surrounding community's quality of life might also be impacted negatively. Economic impact is another area of concern.

In this section, we will be examining the following means through which development may impact the environment:

- Air quality and air emissions
- Water quality and water resources
- Landscape and land contamination
- Biodiversity and natural resources

- Waste management
- Historic and cultural resources
- Socioeconomic impacts

Air quality and air emissions

Large developments cause air pollutants to be released into the atmosphere during the construction and operation phases. These include toxic gases like benzene and other hydrocarbons that can be carcinogenic. Another category are greenhouse gas emissions, particularly carbon dioxide that scientists have linked to climate change. The key contributor to greenhouse gas emissions is the burning of fossil fuels that has significantly increased the amount of carbon dioxide in the atmosphere.

Each jurisdiction has legislation that outlines air quality standards that need to be maintained. For example, in the United States, under the auspices of the Clean Air Act, the Environmental Protection Agency (EPA) sets National Ambient Air Quality Standards for six pollutants: Carbon Monoxide, Lead, Nitrogen Dioxide, Ozone, Particle Pollution and Sulphur Dioxide (see: https://www.epa.gov/criteria-air-pollutants/naaqs-table).

The types and amount of air pollutants need to be quantified and assessed. Detailed emission inventories and dispersion modelling is carried out as part of this process. Following this, mitigation measures are developed to keep air quality levels within the acceptable range.

Water quality and water resources

The impact to the naturally occurring water sources in an area needs to be considered. These water sources could be in the form of rivers, lakes and wetlands.

Many large sites have naturally occurring water bodies and streams. Buildings and infrastructure on such sites have to carefully consider how to preserve them or have minimum negative impact on them.

Developments could impact the water quality of surrounding water bodies and groundwater in terms of pollutants as a result of storm water runoff. This could occur both during the construction and operation of the development.

Monitoring needs to be done by collecting water samples from the drains and discharge points to ensure that stormwater runoff from the drains in the development meet the water quality standards of that jurisdiction.

Landscape and land contamination

When buildings are constructed as part of a large development, clearance of the natural landscape and disruption to the existing landform and natural features of the site is often an inevitable part of the process.

This affects more than just the visual quality of the landscape. The clearance of vegetation could result in soil erosion. The drainage of the site could also be affected, resulting in increased risk and or occurrence of flooding. Generally, the disturbance of topsoil causes the loss of arable land. And while construction is taking place, the chemicals used could then result in soil and groundwater contamination.

Biodiversity and natural resources

With an increase in the global population and urbanisation, there is a pressing need to preserve the natural environment. Loss of habitats for flora and fauna will have detrimental effects for biodiversity and the ecosystem.

Where possible, natural areas should be left undeveloped, particularly if there are endangered species residing in that habitat. Instead, development should first be considered for previously disturbed land and the restricted development of natural lands to be kept to the minimum. Where impacts are unavoidable, mitigation measures like the relocation of affected species to another habitat or a restored habitat should be considered.

Waste management

Large developments generate many types of waste. These various types need to be identified, particularly hazardous waste. A plan needs to be put in place to prevent the indiscriminate disposal or discharge of waste. This plan needs to consider both the construction stage as well as the operations stage.

At the construction stage, there will be construction waste that need to be disposed of. This waste could be the result of the construction process, packing material, or waste generated by the workers on site. This waste should be minimised or recycled. Wastewater and sewerage from the site need to be processed before discharge. Some brownfield sites have contaminated soil that need to be disposed of in a responsible manner.

The operations phase also needs to be considered, as does waste generated over the lifespan of the development. The various waste streams need to be considered. Facilities and infrastructure to facilitate recycling and the effective disposal of waste need to be put in place.

Historic and cultural resources

There is a need to protect historic places. For example, buildings where important events took place or where people of historic significance resided. Some sites also have cultural significance; an example of such places are graveyards. The resting places of the deceased are considered sacred in many communities and they are also a rich source of history and information about the community.

The removal of such places and sites result in the loss of cultural heritage for the community. Even if the building was relocated or rebuilt, the historical integrity of the place would be compromised. These buildings provide a link from the present day to the past. Historic buildings provide a sense of place and imbibe a location with unique characteristics.

Socioeconomic impacts

The socioeconomic impacts of a project also need to be considered. These impacts include direct economic impacts, indirect economic impacts, impact on housing and services etc.

Large developments bring employment for the region. For example, an airport has many businesses on site, and that generates a large number of jobs. Then there are direct economic effects, like employment and the buying of services from businesses in the region, as well as indirect economic effects created by the spending from employees that work at the airport.

There are, of course, negative aspects that also need to be considered. For example, there could be loss of homes because of the expansion of the airport to build a new runway.

Others

Each site and development has its own unique characteristics. This results in a special combination of environmental impact that might not be present at another site and or development.

For example, noise is a special category for airports because of flying aircraft affecting neighbouring areas as they land, take off and overfly neighbouring areas.

Apart from negative impacts like noise pollution, there might also be the presence of endangered species in a particular area to consider. For example, in Hong Kong the pink dolphin needs special attention, and is thus a point of consideration in developments that may affect their habitats directly or otherwise. And in some places, the clearance of a particular site could have very disruptive impacts on a particular industry which would warrant closer study.

Environmental legislation

In order to address the environmental impacts of development and human activity, there are environmental laws to address each aspect

of environmental impact. Examples of such laws are outlined in the
following table.

Table 7.1   Examples of environmental impacts of development and the
corresponding environmental laws enacted in the USA and Singapore to
manage them.

	Environmental Issue	Examples of US Federal Environmental Laws	Examples of Singapore Environmental Laws
1	Air quality and air emissions	Clean Air Act of 1970	Environmental Protection and Management Act, 2002
2	Water quality and water resources	Clean Water Act, Section 404 Wild and Scenic Rivers Act of 1968	Public Utilities Act, 2002 Sewerage and Drainage Act, 2001
3	Landscape and land contamination	Farmland Protection Policy Act	Parks and Trees Act, 2006
4	Biodiversity and natural resources	Endangered Species Act of 1973	Wild Animals and Birds Act, 2000 Parks and Trees Act, 2006
5	Waste management	Resource Conservation and Recovery Act of 1976	Environmental Protection and Management Act, 2002 Environmental Public Health Act, 2002
6	Historic and cultural issues	National Historic Preservation Act of 1966	–

	Environmental Issue	Examples of US Federal Environmental Laws	Examples of Singapore Environmental Laws
7	Socioeconomic impacts	Uniform Relocation Assistance and Real Property Acquisition Policies Act of 1970	–
8	Others	Aviation Safety and Noise Abatement Act of 1979	–

7.2 Essential #7b – Learning the key aspects of the environmental impact assessment process

Environmental impact assessment

What is an Environmental Impact Assessment (EIA)? It is a tool for assessing the environmental impact of a development project. The environmental impacts are identified, predicted and evaluated, and mitigation measures are proposed. Alternatives for the development are also considered. The public and affected parties are informed and consulted before a final decision is taken for the development.

There are different definitions for EIA but they all have the characteristics mentioned above. For example, the International Association for Impact Assessment (IAIA) and the UK Institute of Environmental Assessment (IEA) define EIAs as:

"The process of identifying, predicting, evaluating, and mitigating the biophysical, social, and other relevant effects of development proposals prior to major decisions being taken and commitments made."

Environmental impact assessment legislation

In most countries, there is legislation outlining what an EIA is, what projects require an EIA and the EIA process.

The projects requiring an EIA are typically for facilities with large sites that have a high environmental impact like nuclear power stations and large airports. The format of the EIA, level of public engagement, requirements and conditions for an approval or permit to move forward with the development are typically outlined in the EIA legislation. Hence, the legislation and accompanying guidelines and interpretations have to be carefully scrutinised and followed in order to have the EIA process completed in a timely manner.

An example of EIA legislation is the United States National Environmental Policy Act (NEPA) enacted in 1969. Projects by the United States Federal government or projects that have federal funding are required to comply with NEPA, the process that agencies are required to follow. Projects that require a full EIA are defined. The public is informed about such projects and is consulted and involved. These ensure that all options and the public's input are considered before a decision is taken.

Another example is the Hong Kong Environmental Impact Assessment (EIA) Ordinance, Cap. 499 that is administered by the Environmental Protection Department (EPD). Some provisions of the ordinance include the following:

- Section 7(1) of the ordinance requires exhibiting of the EIA report.
- Section 8(3) of the ordinance requires approval of the EIA report.
- Section 10(1) of the ordinance requires the developer to apply for an Environmental Permit.

In line with involving the public and making the information publicly available, approved EIA reports and environmental permits are available for viewing at the EPD website.

For countries that are part of the European Union (EU), the Environmental Impact Assessment (EIA) Directive 85/337/EEC (1985) requires an EIA to be carried out for a range of defined projects, both public and private. Annex I lists the types of projects where EIA is mandatory. Annex II lists the projects where the decision rests with the national governments based on a screening process. There are three key parties in the EU EIA process:

1. **The 'competent authority'** that decides what will be covered in EIA. After receiving information from the developer and the conclusion of the public consultation process, the 'competent authority' makes the decision in regard to the project.
2. **The developer** that provides information to the public and affected parties on the environmental impacts based on the agreed scope of the EIA (in discussions with the 'competent authority'). This ensures that there is a public consultation process.
3. **The public** who are informed of the impacts of the project and consulted. The public must be informed of the development decision and can appeal the decision in the courts.

EIA legislation in Singapore

As seen in the earlier table, Singapore has multiple environmental laws that developers must grapple with. However, the country currently has no mandatory EIA legislation. Instead, the Singapore Government decides if EIAs must be performed on a case-by-case basis.

In recent years, the Singapore government has performed EIAs for various projects. For example, it was reported that an EIA was carried out for the new Tuas port project. However, the report was not made publicly available.

The first EIA to be made publicly available in Singapore is the EIA for Soil Investigation works for the Cross Island Line crossing the Central Catchment Nature Reserve. Initially, it was only made available in hard copy for viewing by appointment. After public feedback to make it more accessible, the EIA reports were uploaded to the Land Transit Authority's website for public viewing. There will be a second phase for the EIA for this project. This EIA will be for the Construction and Operations phase of the project.

The "Mandai eco-tourism hub" project is the second project where the EIA has been made publicly available on the organisation's website. The website also allowed for suggestions and comments to be submitted to Mandai Park Holdings, the project developer. The Mandai project also has an Environmental Advisory Panel for oversight of the mitigation measures proposed in the EIA.

The Singapore Government has also announced that it will be conducting an environmental study for the proposed site of a new public housing development, Tengah New Town, and will be making the findings known to the public.

It can be seen that EIAs are becoming more commonplace in Singapore. The level of public involvement is also increasing with the public release of EIA reports and increased public engagement in terms of seeking public feedback on EIAs of projects like the Mandai project.

EIA process

We will now consider the various phases in the EIA process:

1. Screening
2. Scoping
3. Studying the impacts and mitigation measures
4. Public consultation and decision
5. Implementation

Step 1 – Screening

The first phase of the EIA process is screening. This is done after the project description and listing of possible alternatives have been completed. The key question that needs to be asked is whether the environmental impacts that will result from the project are significant enough that it needs to undergo the EIA process. The EIA legislation and guidelines will outline which types of projects are significant enough to undergo the EIA process. The relevant government authority will make a decision on this based on the submission by the project sponsor.

Step 2 – Scoping

Once it has been decided that the project needs to undergo the EIA process, scoping — which defines what areas of impact need to be studied as part of the EIA process — must be carried out. The EIA process is costly and requires time and resources. Scoping helps to focus these resources on the necessary areas of study and creates an outline for these specific areas.

Step 3 – Studying the impacts and mitigation measures

A plan needs to be drawn up to study the environmental impacts. This involves creating a baseline for the areas of study identified in the earlier scoping exercise. The study typically needs to be carried out over an entire year as there are seasonal changes in the environmental that need to be captured for completeness.

This is followed by a process of predicting the environmental impacts as a result of the project. The impact of the construction activities and operation of the buildings on the environment is then assessed. Various alternatives for the project are considered including a no-build alternative to provide a basis for comparison.

Possible mitigation measures are considered to reduce the impact of the development. Of particular importance is the consideration of areas where there is high environment impact, and the determining of means to eliminate or reduce the impact through mitigation measures. This will at least reduce the environmental impacts to an acceptable level.

Step 4 – Public consultation and decision

The results of the EIA study are then presented for public consultation. This is an integral part of the EIA process and the public (including all stakeholders) are invited to provide feedback. This public consultation process allows all stakeholders a place to air their concerns and for these concerns to be addressed. The needs of all parties are considered in an integrated and comprehensive manner. The feedback collected becomes part of the final EIA report. After the report is completed, a recommendation is made to the relevant authority for a decision.

This is followed by a final decision on whether the project can proceed, which alternative is chosen as well as the mitigation measures that are to be incorporated into the project during the construction and operations phases of the project.

Step 5 – Implementation

Once the necessary environmental permissions are received, the project can move into the implementation phase. During this phase, the efficacy of the mitigation measures needs to be monitored to ensure that the conditions of the granting of the environmental permit are met and adhered to.

7.3 Stakeholders

Stakeholder engagement is the heart of the EIA process. This ensures that all stakeholders are informed of the project, have an opportunity to voice their concerns and have their feedback incorporated into the development project report.

At the heart of any EIA is the involvement of stakeholders. The sharing of information regarding the project will lead to a collaborative process of solving the problems that present themselves, namely the negative environmental impacts.

Who are the stakeholders? Stakeholders are people or groups that are affected and impacted by a project, either directly or indirectly. It includes people who have an interest in the project and are able to influence the project in either a positive or negative way.

The stakeholders to be involved in the EIA can be determined by the requirements of the associated legislation, the developer's policies and guidelines, and international best practices.

Having a defined stakeholder engagement process allows information about the project to be disseminated to all concerned in a structured manner that is both timely and effective. It provides platforms for stakeholders to voice their concerns and opinions. This allows their views to be documented in a systematic fashion so that they can be addressed and considered in the decision-making process. Also, the opportunity to dialogue could lead to enhanced understanding between the project sponsor and the stakeholders and among the various stakeholders. This helps to get everyone on the same page in terms of the facts as well as establish what the points of agreement and disagreement are, so that the best way forward can be forged.

Examples of stakeholders are as follows:

- Green groups in situations when there is disturbance to flora and fauna.
- Business and Home owners when land acquisition for a large project is involved.

There are various ways to engage stakeholders. For example, this could be done in the form of exhibitions to present information about the project to the community. Staff present can answer any questions that visitors have regarding the project. Information can be posted online for stakeholders to assess and comment on.

7.4   Case study: Hong Kong International Airport Three Runway System

We will now examine the case study of the Hong Kong International Airport Three Runway Project.

In response to increasing traffic at Hong Kong International Airport (HKIA), the Airport Authority Hong Kong (AAHK) decided to launch the HKIA Three Runway System (TRS) Project. The airport currently has two runways that are approaching maximum capacity, and so, it makes sense that a third runway and accompanying terminal facilities are needed.

The Environmental Impact Assessment Ordinance is administered by the Environmental Protection Department (EPD) of the Government of the Hong Kong Special Administrative Region. The website shows the following information for the project:

- Expansion of Hong Kong International Airport into a Three-Runway System
- Project Profile (PP-469/2012)
- Study Brief issued (ESB-250/2012)
- EIA Report (AEIAR-185/2014)
- Current Environmental Permit Held (EP-489/2014)
- Link to Project Website and Environmental Monitoring and Audit Data

The full reports are available for download from the EPD website.

Enough time needs to be set aside for the project planning and project approval. The timeline for the whole project is 11 years. The first three years are set aside for project planning and project approval. This includes conducting the EIA studies and initial design work, studying funding options and securing the necessary statutory approvals including the environmental permit. The remaining eight years are for the detailed design and construction works, land reclamation works and the commissioning of the runway system.

Table 7.2   Timeline from project planning and approval phase of the Hong Kong International Airport Three Runway Project to commencement of construction.

Year	Year	Description
Year 1	2012	Mar 2012 – The Three Runway System (TRS) is adopted as the development option for planning purposes approved in principle by Government. May 2012 – Project Profile submitted to Government by Airport Authority of Hong Kong (AAHK) Aug 2012 – EIA Study Brief issued by Government
Year 2	2013	Aug 2013 – Public exhibition and forum
Year 3	2014	Jun 2014 – EIA Report published Nov 2014 – EIA Report and Environmental Permit approved

Year	Year	Description
Year 4	2015	Sep 2015 – Airport Authority announces financial arrangement for TRS
Year 5	2016	Apr 2016 – Government approves draft outlines for zoning plan and reclamation related to TRS Aug 2016 – Construction of TRS begins

Extracted from HKAA new releases

The AAHK has also been reaching out to their stakeholders. Broad engagement with the public has been done through exhibitions, a project website (www.threerunwaysystem.com) and publications in the form of newsletters and leaflets. In addition to this, there has been targeted outreach to three groups: technical experts, community leaders and students. Four Technical Briefing Groups centred around environmental issues have also been set up to look into specific project-related environmental challenges, namely: air quality, Chinese white dolphins, fisheries and marine ecology, and noise. To engage the community, five Community Liaison Groups representing the districts near the airport were formed. Student engagement takes the form of visits to the airport and briefings to them. All in all, more than 600 engagement activities in the form of briefings, seminars, visits and meetings have been conducted and this is expected to continue for the duration of the project.

For the TRS project, 12 aspects of environmental impacts were examined:

1. Air Quality
2. Noise
3. Ecology (including the Chinese White Dolphins)
4. Fisheries
5. Health Impact Assessment (in terms of air emissions and aircraft noise)
6. Hazards to Human Life
7. Water Quality
8. Sewerage and Sewage Treatment
9. Waste Management

10. Land Contamination
11. Landscape and Visual
12. Cultural Heritage

The following is HKIA's statement regarding the EIA:

> "We are firmly committed to carry out the EIA process in a highly prudent, transparent and professional manner, and to exploring all possible ways to avoid, minimise, mitigate and compensate for any potential environmental impacts that may arise."

The EIA Study Team is made up of the following consultants and experts:

Table 7.3   Consultants in the TRS EIA Study Team.

	Area of Responsibility	Name of Consultant/Expert
1	EIA Lead Consultant	Mott MacDonald
2	EIA Review Consultant	ERM
3	Air Quality Consultant	Arup
4	Aircraft Noise Consultant	URS
5	Health Impact Experts	Prof Wong Tze Wai, Bernard Berry
6	Chinese White Dolphin Experts	Dr Bernd Wursig, Dr Thomas Jefferson

The team worked closely with the client (AAHK) and the Scheme Design Consultants (Mott MacDonald, Atkins, and AECOM).

For each area of environmental impact, a survey of the existing situation must be conducted to create a baseline. This requires experts and resources. Oftentimes, the survey will be done over the period of one year in order to account for the seasons and variations through a typical year. Based on the scheme-design for the project, the impacts are listed, and mitigation measures are proposed for impacts that cannot be eliminated. Both the construction and operation phases of the development have to be considered. With mitigation measures, the environmental impacts are brought to "acceptable" levels or "as low as reasonably practicable".

The EIA for TRS had more than 250 measures to deal with the potential environmental impacts. Examples of key measures include the following:

- The establishment of a new marine park as a sanctuary for the Chinese White Dolphins.
- The restriction of ferry speeds in order to reduce disturbance to marine life.
- The assignment of one runway to be on standby mode at night, to reduce the effects of runway noise on neighbouring residents.
- The proposal of the Horizontal Directional Drilling construction method for the building of the fuel pipeline, in order to reduce the disturbance to the seabed.
- The proposal to use a non-dredging method for the formation of the land platform for the new runway, to minimise the disturbance to contaminated mud pits in the area.
- The deployment of electric vehicles during the operations phase to reduce air polluting emissions at the airport.

The EIA report for the Hong Kong International Airport Three Runway System was published in June 2014. In November 2014, this EIA Report was approved, and the Environmental Permit was issued by the Hong Kong Environmental Protection Department (EPD).

References

Airport Authority Hong Kong (2018), "Three-Runway System", available at: https://www.threerunwaysystem.com/en/ (accessed 12 Jul 2018)

Ashford, N. J., Mumayiz, S., & Wright, P. H. (2011). *Airport engineering: planning, design, and development of 21st century airports*. John Wiley & Sons.

European Commission (2018), "Environmental Impact Assessment" available at: http://ec.europa.eu/environment/eia/eia-legalcontext.htm (accessed 10 Jul 2018)

Hong Kong Environment Protection Department (2018), "Environment Impact Assessment Ordinance – Expansion of Hong Kong International Airport into a Three-Runway System", available at: https://www.epd.gov.hk/eia/english/alpha/aspd_651.html (accessed 12 Jul 2018)

Land Transport Authority (2018), "Cross Island Line – Environmental Impact Assessment", available at: https://www.lta.gov.sg/content/ltaweb/en/public-transport/projects/cross-island-line.html (accessed 12 Jul 2018)

Mandai Project (2018), "Developing Sensitively – Environmental Impact Assessment", available at: https://www.mandai.com/development (accessed 12 Jul 2018)

National Environment Agency (2018), "Climate Action", available at: https://www.nea.gov.sg/index/climate-action (accessed 1 Oct 2018)

Noble, B. F. (2010). *Introduction to environmental impact assessment: a guide to principles and practice.* Don Mills, Ont.: Oxford University Press.

CHAPTER 8

Capital Improvement Planning

In this chapter, you will learn about the following:

1. Capital improvement planning

2. Essential #8 – Learning the key aspects of the capital improvement planning process and how to put together a capital improvement plan for a large facility

3. CIP Process step 1 – Creating a list of potential projects

4. CIP Process step 2 – Gathering information for each project

5. CIP Process step 3 – Prioritising the projects

6. CIP Process step 4 – Finalising the list of projects

7. Case study: Singapore Government Budget

Essential #8

Learn the key aspects of the capital improvement planning process and how to put together a capital improvement plan for a large facility.

Have you ever wondered how decisions are made in selecting new building projects in an organisation? If you are the chief executive of an airport, how would you decide what capital projects to approve?

This chapter seeks to help the reader learn how to administer the capital improvement planning (CIP) process. It goes through the various terms used in the CIP process, how lists of potential projects are created, how to create evaluation criteria for the selection process, and how the allocation of financial resources for capital improvement are determined.

The Singapore Government Development Budget is discussed in this chapter as a case study.

8.1 Capital improvement planning

Capital Improvement Planning is done on an annual basis and details out what capital expenditure items will be carried out in the coming years.

Buildings are unique because they typically take more than a year to construct, with the project spending profile spanning over a few financial years before it is completed.

Let us first look at what are capital costs, capital improvement projects, and capital budgets and who manages the capital improvement process.

Capital costs and capital improvement projects

Cotts (2007) defines "Capital costs" as "the costs of acquiring, substantially improving, expanding, changing the functional use of, or replacing a building or building system".

A building is a real asset and has a value over many years. Other examples of capital costs are the purchase of new vehicles and costly equipment like computer servers. The definition of capital costs varies between organisations. For some organisations, the value has to be more than US$10,000 in order to be a capital cost, while others might have it pegged at a higher or lower value.

Capital improvement projects often have a duration of more than one year. It includes construction projects, large mechanical and electrical equipment, IT equipment and vehicles. Examples of capital improvement projects are new buildings and infrastructure, and major renovations to existing facilities.

Capital budgets

Budgets are financial plans that are reviewed and revised annually. Most people are familiar with operations budgets that are used for daily and monthly expenses in an organisation over a one-year period. The capital budget differs from this as it deals with expenditures that are related to capital improvement.

Capital spending for projects take place over more than one year. It is long-term and sometimes called a development budget. This is in contrast to an operating budget that involves the purchase of goods and services within one financial year which would be considered short-term. For example, the development of a new school building will be under the capital budget as it will take 3 to 4 years to plan, design and build, before it is ready to be handed over to the school principal and his team to operate.

Organisations like universities and airports own and build a lot of assets. There is always a need to construct new buildings or renovate existing ones. This capital expenditure needs to be planned carefully to optimise the financial resources of the organisation.

Who manages the capital improvement planning process?

A facility manager of a large organisation should be able to manage a small capital improvement programme. If it becomes a large capital improvement programme, there will be a need for a dedicated staff or separate division to handle the capital projects. This Projects division may report directly to the chief executive of the organisation. The rules for the capital improvement programme and budget are made by the finance department. For better control and accountability, there is typically a capital review board that is responsible for gathering requirements, reviewing and prioritising capital projects.

Many capital planning managers stumble into their roles. There is no formal training for it. Some have a background in finance and are trained as financial managers or accountants. They work in the organisation's finance division and 'stumble' into capital improvement when they are tasked to manage the organisation's capital budget.

Others have a background and experience in engineering and project management. They 'stumble' into the role because of their knowledge and experience in capital improvement projects. They are involved in the capital improvement process, providing information to the finance department regarding capital improvement projects.

The staff from the projects or engineering divisions are more focused on the projects that go into the capital improvement plan effort while staff from the finance department are more focused on the financial aspects, like where the funding is coming from and ensuring that all the financial rules are adhered to.

Typically, staff with financial backgrounds would be responsible for the capital improvement programme in the organisation. However, they lack building domain knowledge, and this creates a gap for built environment sector professionals like project managers and engineers to fill. After establishing themselves in built environment sector jobs for five to ten years, and learning how buildings are designed and constructed, a career as a capital programme manager could be the next step for young professionals. Other useful skills to have would be financial management, budgeting, project cost estimating and project scheduling.

8.2   Essential #8 – Learning the key aspects of the capital improvement planning process and how to put together a capital improvement plan for a large facility

The capital improvement planning process takes place annually. It is managed by the finance division with input from the Projects division of an organisation. The end product of this process is the capital improvement plan that contains the information of the capital improvement projects that will be carried out for the year.

Importance of the capital improvement planning (CIP) process

The CIP process is important for the following reasons. Firstly, the CIP process ensures that the facilities of the organisation are improved to an adequate level. It identifies the projects that will expand the capacity of the facilities or renovate the facilities to maintain the quality of the facilities.

Secondly, the CIP process ensures that the organisation's funds are spent in a prudent manner. Since there are multiple projects that need to be executed, it focuses the organisation's limited funds and manpower onto projects that are important to the organisation.

Finally, the CIP process involves all the stakeholders in a structured manner. Without the intervention of the CIP process, it is normal for the various divisions in an organisation to feel that their capital improvement projects are more important and advocate for their projects to be done first. Likewise, for larger projects, there are multiple stakeholders who will push for their projects to be started first. The planning process provides a platform for all these stakeholders to be involved at the appropriate times in the process.

Steps in the capital improvement planning process

These are the major steps in an organisation's capital improvement planning process:

1. Create a list of potential projects
   - Identify needs (from business plan and master plan); project requests from staff
   - Project request review by originating division manager and planning staff
2. Gathering information for each project
   - Identify funding sources/potential funding sources for the projects
3. Prioritise projects
   - Relevant staff prioritise projects based on set prioritisation criteria
4. Finalise the list of projects and the Capital Improvement Plan
   - Prepare shortlist of recommended projects
   - Finalise list of all projects for inclusion into the capital improvement plan

Each step of the capital improvement process will be explained in detail in the following sections.

8.3   CIP Process step 1 – Create a list of potential projects

The first thing that needs to be done in capital planning is to create a list of potential projects. This is done by the staff designated as the capital planner. The sources of potential projects are the organisation's plans and project requests from staff.

Potential projects are reviewed by the originating division manager and planning staff before being accepted for consideration in the CIP process. Information about the potential project needs to be collected and entered into a project database.

Source of potential projects – Organisation's plans (strategic plan, facility master plan)

The organisation's plans like the strategic plan and facility master plan need to be reviewed for potential projects. There is a strong connection between the strategic plan and the capital improvement plan. For example, in a university that is introducing residential colleges as a strategic thrust to integrate learning with student life, capital projects to build residential colleges will become part of the capital improvement plan of the university.

The facility master plan also considers the strategic plan when it is being developed. Hence, many potential projects can be identified from the master plan and activated for implementation through the capital improvement plan. As mentioned in the earlier chapter on master planning, the development needs will often be divided into short-term, medium-term and long-term. The short-term projects identified in the master plan will typically be the first to be implemented as part of the capital improvement plan.

Source of potential projects – Project requests from staff

Another way of identifying potential projects is by collecting inputs from staff and managers. A standardised form for requesting projects is filled in by relevant staff and managers. Potential projects could also be generated by the facility planner. These are compiled into a preliminary list.

Requirements need to be collected from all groups. Sometimes, this is done through the various managers, in other cases, this can be collected directly from the requestor.

Examples of capital improvement projects at airports

Let us consider this in the context of an airport. The following are some examples of airport capital improvement projects. These projects could be organised into the following categories: airside, terminal, and landside.

Table 8.1   Examples of airport capital improvement projects (by category).

	Category	Examples of Capital Projects
1	Airside	Building a new runway or adding new taxiways. It could also include rehabilitation of an existing runway, replace of the airport perimeter fence or expansion of the aircraft parking apron.
2	Terminal	Terminal expansions to cater to growing traffic could be an example of a terminal capital project. Adding baggage carousels and adding security checkpoint lanes are other examples. It could also be the upgrading or replacement of systems like the security system, air conditioning system or fire protection system.
3	Landside	Construction of new parking lots, garages and consolidated rental car centres, rehabilitation of the roadways and improving signage.

The following are some examples of project requests from airport staff.

- The Building Maintenance division will be able to identify the large equipment that are due for replacement because the equipment have reached the end of their lifespan or are constantly breaking down.
- The Security division will be aware of security project needs. For example, there might be a need to replace fences. Or there might be a government grant available that could advance a project for hardening the perimeter fencing of the airport.
- The Information Systems division could also be a source of capital improvement projects. Examples of new projects could be the installation of a new fibre networks for redundancy and increased resilience. There could be a need to buy new servers and add additional security cameras to the terminal building or airport campus.
- The Operations division might request for the repaving of the airport perimeter road network that is reaching the end of its useful life.

8.4   CIP Process step 2 – Gathering information for each project

In addition to compiling a list of potential capital improvement projects for consideration, the following information are required for each potential project.

- Name of project
- Type of project
- Description of project
- Justification for project
- Estimated cost for project
- Potential funding source
- Project schedule

Name, type and description of project

When naming projects, project titles should be clear and precise so that they are self-explanatory to the reader. However, they also need to be broad enough to accommodate any minor changes that occur during the scoping and design process as the project proceeds.

There are various ways to organise the list of capital projects. They can be organised geographically, or by categories — like new buildings, renovation and improvement projects, and new equipment (i.e. Mechanical and Electrical, Information Technology, or Vehicular assets).

A description of the project needs to be provided. For example, the number of floors in the building, floor area of the building, the rooms in the building, furniture and furnishing, etc. The level of detail needs to be sufficient for a rough order-of-magnitude cost estimate to be done for the potential project.

Justification for project

To properly rank the potential project relative to the other potential projects, justification for the project needs to be provided. Another way would be to think of what would occur if the project was not carried out.

There are a number of reasons why a project is needed. At an airport, examples will include the following:

- Safety: Airfield safety is critical. A runway resurfacing project can be justified on the grounds of runway safety as a worn-out runway surface could affect the landing and take-off operations in rainy weather.
- Regulatory requirement: Airport security regulations could require enhancements the security checkpoint area. Citing the relevant regulatory requirement would be a good justification for the project.
- Operational requirement: A growing airport would require more baggage carousels to cope with the increase in arriving passengers. The addition of additional baggage carousels would be justified as an operational requirement as it is necessary for the smooth operations of the airport.

Cost estimate and funding sources

The cost estimates for potential projects can be done by in-house staff who are familiar with the airport projects. An alternative is to outsource this to a consultant. Estimating costs at this point is difficult because of the minimal details available at this point. For example, cost estimates will be done based on projected floor area.

There are a number of funding sources for capital projects. They can be funded from the profits of the company. For organisations that have insufficient funds for capital investment, loans can be taken from financial institutions or bonds can be issued by the organisation. Another funding source is in the form of grants from government agencies or private grant making organisations like foundations.

Project schedule – Time taken to execute project

As mentioned in the earlier part of the chapter, construction projects are a multi-year endeavour. Table 8.2 shows the activities that occur yearly for a typical construction project, e.g. a new secondary school. Planning and design activities including procurement occupy the first three years with construction taking the next two years, concluding in the defect liability period in the final sixth year.

Table 8.2   Timeline for a typical construction project.

	Year	Activities
1	Year 1	Bring PM on board, scope the project, request for consultancy services, select consultant
2	Year 2	Design
3	Year 3	Prepare tender drawings, tender and award
4	Year 4	Construction
5	Year 5	Construction
6	Year 6	Defects Liability period

8.5 CIP Process step 3 – Prioritise the projects

Potential projects are then prioritised, often using predetermined evaluation criteria. This is typically done in a group with representatives from the various stakeholders present. A committee needs to be set up to prioritise the list of potential projects. The composition of the committee could include the managers of the Operations, Maintenance, Information Technology, Planning, Projects, and Finance divisions. It is essential that there is representation from key workgroups. Once this is completed, a shortlist of proposed projects will be forwarded to the executive team for consideration.

Prioritisation criteria

Criteria that are considered in the prioritisation of capital projects include the following:

- safety
- regulatory
- essential maintenance, preventative maintenance
- user needs
- operational considerations
- environmental concerns

Safety is normally on the top of any prioritisation list as danger to human life is not acceptable so capital projects to address safety issues need to be carried out as soon as possible. Closely associated to this is regulatory issues, these capital projects also tend to make it to the top of the list as failure to comply with regulations will result in penalties like fines or the inability to carry on operations because of licensing requirements.

Maintenance projects can be divided into essential and preventative. Essential maintenance projects include rehabilitating equipment and assets that are breaking down or that have reached the end of their useful lives. These tend to take precedence over preventive maintenance projects. Preventative maintenance projects prolong the life of the asset and reduce the incidence of breakdowns.

User needs are important particularly in service-oriented facilities like hotels and airports. For example, projects to enhance restrooms and amenities will be prioritised for airports that want to maintain a high level of customer service for their passengers.

Operational considerations refer to projects that will enhance the operations of the facility. For example, a project like an enlarged loading dock will improve the operations of a shopping centre by relieving congestion at the loading dock during peak hours.

Environmental concerns, particularly in communities where environmental concerns are paramount, will advance projects that will enhance the sustainability of the facility. Examples of such projects are the installation of solar panels on the flat roofs of existing buildings in the facility.

There is a high level of subjectivity in the prioritisation criteria. It varies from organisation to organisation and might also involve organisational politics. To get capital projects approved and placed on the capital plan, it is important to link the project to a regulatory requirement or business need. Another strategy would be to find grants and money for desired projects as projects with external funding would be more attractive to execute.

8.6   CIP Process step 4 – Finalising the list of projects

A shortlist of the projects to move ahead with will be decided upon by the senior management of the organisation. This will be constrained by the available capital in the organisation or the ability of the organisation to raise funds for the projects. Approval of the capital improvement plan is by the organisation's board. For example, at an airport operated by a municipal government, this approval will be the City Council.

Once approved, the projects are compiled into the Capital Improvement Plan report. At a minimum, the Capital Improvement Plan report contains the following:

- List of projects
- Budget for each project
- Estimated amount to be spent for each year
- Funding source

The Capital Improvement Plan report is typically a five-year plan that is updated annually. It shows more than one year of capital expenditure because building projects last for more than a year and there is a need to see the multi-year financial implications of committing to a project. Smaller projects can be grouped into a larger single 'improvements' project item. The level of detail varies with the requirements of the finance department.

8.7 Case study: Singapore Government Budget

One of the key end products of the capital improvement planning process is the Capital Budget. Let us explore this by examining the Singapore Government Budget.

The Singapore Government has an annual budget process to plan for government revenues and expenditures. The financial year for the Singapore Government runs from 1 April to 31 March. The budget for each year is available on the Singapore Ministry of Finance Budget website.

The estimates for expenditure for each of government ministry and organ of the state are listed. In terms of expenditure, there are two large categories. The first is "running costs" which are the operating expenditures for each government entity while the second is "development estimates" which are the capital expenditures for public projects.

Example: Development estimates for the top five ministries

An examination of the Budget in 2016 gives a sense of the type of large public capital projects in Singapore. The proposed 2016 budget was S$32 billion. Table 8.3 shows the highest development estimates (for capital projects) for the following government entities in that year:

Table 8.3   Top five (highest cost) development estimates for capital projects by government ministries in Singapore in 2016.

SNo	Ministry	Development Estimates (in SGD millions)	Facilities
1	Ministry of National Development	10,992	E.g. Public Housing
2	Ministry of Transport	9,459	Transport facilities. E.g. Rail, Airport, Seaport.
3	Ministry of Trade and Industry	5,662	E.g. Industrial parks
4	Ministry of Health	1,797	Healthcare facilities. E.g. Hospitals, Nursing Homes, Polyclinics
5	Ministry of the Environment and Water Resources	704	E.g. Sewers, Drains.

Source: Singapore Budget 2016.

Example: Ministry of Health projects

Let us now examine one of the ministries to see the specific projects that are being built. Table 8.4 shows some of the larger projects under the Ministry of Health in 2016.

Table 8.4 Large projects under the Ministry of Health in 2016.

SNo	Ministry of Health	Projects (some examples)
1	Hospitals	Yishun Community Hospital, Ng Teng Fong General Hospital and Jurong Community Hospital, Communicable Diseases Centre, Sengkang General Hospital, Outram Community Hospital, NUH Centre for Oral Health and Service Block, NUHS Utility Plant, CGH Integrated Building, SGH Carpark and Master Plan
2	Nursing Homes	Taman Jurong, Woodlands Crescent, Tampines North, Assisi Hospice
3	Polyclinics	Punggol, Bedok, Admiralty Medical Centre, Pioneer, Yishun + Senior Care Centre, Ang Mo Kio + Senior Care Centre

Source: Singapore Budget 2016

Project cost estimates and expenditures

The following are the categories in Table 8.5 for the development of Sengkang General Hospital:

- Total Project Cost
- Actual Expenditure up to the end of FY2013
- Actual FY2014
- Estimated FY2015
- Revised FY2015
- Estimated FY2016

The estimates are provided by the project management offices of the various government ministries. As shown in the earlier section, information about potential projects need to be collected. The estimated "total project cost" needs to be provided for input into the final capital budget.

The project cashflow also needs to be estimated on a yearly basis. The length of the project needs to be estimated by drawing up a project schedule with planning, design and construction phases. For example, a school project could take about 3.5 years with half a year of planning, one year of design and two years of construction.

Next, the amount of money that will be spent for each phase is estimated. Most of the money is spent during the construction phase and is paid out in monthly progress payments to the contractor. The next biggest amount are the consultant fees that are largely paid out during the design phase with a portion paid out for consultant services during the construction phase. The payments are typically tied to milestones like the completion of schematic design drawings, design development drawings and construction documents for calling tenders.

Example: Sengkang General Hospital

From the detailed information provided in the government budget, the largest projects (in terms of cost) can be identified by looking at the "Total project cost". In Budget 2016, the largest project under the Ministry of Health was Sengkang General Hospital which had a total project cost of S$1.35 billion.

Using the example of Sengkang General Hospital, let us see what can be gleaned from the information available.

Table 8.5   Development expenditure for Sengkang General Hospital project.

	Sengkang General Hospital	S$	% of Total Project cost
1	Total Project Cost	1,353,202,200	
2	Actual Expenditure up to the end of FY2013	31,442,188	2.3%
3	Actual FY2014	74,197,984	5.5%
4	Estimated FY2015	225,369,800	

	Sengkang General Hospital	S$	% of Total Project cost
5	Revised FY2015	142,789,900	10.6%
6	Estimated FY2016	532,320,800	39.3%

Source: Singapore Government Budget 2016

Projects are multi-year endeavours. It is funded gradually year by year rather than all in one year.

Comparing the years, you can see that FY2016 will see the construction of the hospital in full swing, with 39% of the total project cost spent in that year compared to smaller amounts in FY2015 and FY2014. It can also be seen that about 58% of the project cost will be spent in FY2016 and before, while the remaining 42% will be spent in FY2017 and after. Hence, the budget provides useful information on the spend rate for each project for future cash flow projections.

When reading the information, it is important to note that the total project cost for some projects are still in flux particularly in the early stages of the project when the building has yet to be built. Also, for some projects, the number shown is not the total project cost but just the government's portion, with the rest paid for by a private party.

As can be seen from large difference between line 5, "Estimated FY2015", and line 6, "Revised FY2015", it is difficult to accurately estimate the amount of expenditure each financial year. This is because progress of work can be difficult to predict with issues like an extended design phase because of change in requirements or slow progress on site because of weather related issues.

References

City of Austin (2018), "Capital Planning Office", available at: http://www. austintexas.gov/department/capital-planning/about (accessed 12 Jul 2018)
City of Austin Capital Planning Office (2018), "The Austin Around You – Capital Improvement Program Overview", available at: http://austintexas.gov/sites/

default/files/files/Capital_Planning/Reports_and_Plans/The_Austin_Around_You_CIP_Overview.pdf (accessed 12 Jul 2018)

Cotts, D. G., & Rondeau, E. P. (2004). *The Facility Manager's Guide to Finance and Budgeting*. Amacom Books.

Iowa State University (2018), "Capital Planning Process – Pre-Planning" available at: https://www.fpm.iastate.edu/planning/capital_planning_process/pre_planning.asp (accessed 12 Jul 2018)

National University of Singapore Office of Estate Development (2018), "Our Projects", available at: http://www.nus.edu.sg/oed/index.html (accessed 12 Jul 2018)

Rondeau, E. P., Brown, R. K., & Lapides, P. D. (2012). *Facility management*. John Wiley & Sons.

Singapore Ministry of Finance (2016), "Budget 2016", available at: https://www.singaporebudget.gov.sg/budget_2016/BudgetMeasures/BudgetSummary (accessed 12 Jul 2018)

Singapore Ministry of Finance (2018), "Budget 2018", available at: https://www.singaporebudget.gov.sg/budget_2018/home (accessed 16 Jul 2018)

PART 3
Workplace Planning and Design

CHAPTER 9

Workplace Planning and Design

In this chapter, you will learn about the following:

1. Key trends that are driving change in organisations and the workplace

2. Changes in workspaces, meeting spaces, support spaces and technology

3. Essential #9 – Considerations that must be taken in the planning and design of offices

4. Challenges in implementing a new office concept

5. Coworking spaces

Essential #9

Understand the considerations in the planning and design of workplaces.

The previous chapters considered planning and design at large scales (e.g. building scale and campus scale). This chapter considers planning and design at a smaller scale, specifically office spaces. This chapter also seeks to help the reader consider planning and design in the context of a particular type of facility — offices.

Many people spend at least forty hours a week at their workplace. This accounts for a substantial portion of their time. Hence, it is important that their workplaces are well-planned and well-designed. Another reason is that the layout and design of the workplace can affect a worker's productivity and job satisfaction.

This chapter will focus on workers in an office setting as this is the situation that is most typical. The layout and design of an office is determined by the organisation whose employees occupy the office. The organisation's activities also drive the layout and design of the office.

9.1 Key trends driving change in organisations and the workplace

According to the **Whole Building Design Guide** (WBDG) (2017) there are three key trends that are driving change in organisations and the nature of work:

- Globalisation and increased competition.
- The Information and Communications Technology (ICT) revolution.
- The increasing pace of change resulting from increased competition and the technology revolution.

Globalisation has brought out enhanced competition which has led to companies needing to become leaner. Organisations strive to be 'lean' in a drive to become more competitive, agile and focused on the customer.

Information and Communications Technology (ICT) has progressed rapidly, particularly in the areas of Internet and mobile devices. Technology has drastically altered the nature of work as it has enabled workers to work remotely and still be 'tethered' (connected via the internet) to the organisation.

The pace of change in society and the economy is becoming increasingly rapid. Globalisation and the interconnectedness of the world as a result of the technology revolution are fuelling this rapid change. As people are more connected, there is more communication and more sharing of ideas. Previously, change was slower as it took time for knowledge and information to be shared.

Organisations, as a part of society and the economy, also have to adapt and change. In the private sector, the increased competition has meant that companies have to be more innovative, more efficient, get the best manpower and enable them to produce the best results. The key principles of the 'lean enterprise' as described in the WBDG (2017) are to add value and eliminate waste.

Organisations add value by focusing on activities that are value adding from the perspective of the customer. Organisations strive to remove inefficiencies and activities that are not value adding, particularly in support areas. Key organisational changes have to be made to add value, reduce waste and make the organisation more adaptable to change.

In the face of globalisation, competition, technology revolution and rapid change, there are five ways in which organisations and their workplaces have changed (WBDG, 2017):

- Increased use of teams
- Greater use of dispersed work groups
- Continual reorganisation and restructuring
- The need to reduce costs
- Improve quality of work life to attract and retain staff

Table 9.1 shows how each of the four trends have caused change in the workplace.

Table 9.1   Changes in organisations and their workplaces in response to trends.

	Trend	Increased Use of Teams	Greater Use of Dispersed Work Groups	Continual Reorganisation and Restructuring	Reduce Costs	Improve Quality of Work Life to Attract and Retain Staff
1	Globalisation		Y	Y		
2	Competition	Y		Y	Y	Y
3	Technology Revolution	Y	Y			
4	Rapid Change	Y		Y		

9.2 Changes in workspaces, meeting spaces, support spaces and technology

The physical layout of offices can be divided into different areas: workspaces, meeting spaces and support areas. Technology also needs to be considered as it is an indispensable part of the modern office. Table 9.2 illustrates how organisational changes have caused changes in the physical layout of, as manifested in terms of, workspaces, meeting spaces, support spaces and technology.

Table 9.2   Changes in physical layouts of offices in response to organisation changes.

	Organisational Changes	Workspaces	Meeting Spaces	Support Spaces	Technology
1	Increased use of teams	Smaller and more open. Unassigned. Use of project rooms. Small rooms for individual focus.	More and greater variety.	Lockers for unassigned workspaces.	Mobile support (phones, laptops). Instant messaging, team software solutions.
2	Greater use of dispersed work groups	Use of space beyond office hours.	Technologically enabled meeting spaces.		Video conferencing and computer-based team solutions. Conference calls.
3	Continual reorganisation and restructuring	Standardised and mobile furnishings. Flexible infrastructure to allow for easy reconfiguration.			
4	Reduce costs	Shared or unassigned spaces. Reduced workstation size and increased densities. Increased variety of workspaces to accommodate different types of work.		Centralised filing systems. Off-site storage.	

(Continued)

Table 9.2   (*Continued*)

	Organisational Changes	Workspaces	Meeting Spaces	Support Spaces	Technology
5	Improve quality of work life to attract and retain staff	Equitable access to daylight and views. Equitable allocation of space.		Amenities for stress reduction and relaxation.	

In terms of workspaces, there is a reduction in 'me' space and an increase in 'we' space in response to the need for more space for teamwork. A flatter and more egalitarian organisation structure has resulted in a more open office, where office spaces have become more uniform in terms of size and layout. To be more adaptable, open plan offices tend to be adopted. Desk sizes have also shrunk as the cost of real estate and maintenance have increased. Because of the ability of employees to work remotely, there has been increased experimentation with hot-desking where employees do not have a fixed desk. The workplace is now a multi-dimensional space that supports a diverse range of work activities and different employee behaviours and needs.

There is an increase in the number and variety of meeting spaces. These spaces have become increasingly collaborative with a variety of team spaces for group discussions and team work to happen. As work becomes more ideas-based rather than menial, providing workers with spaces which help idea generation becomes quite critical in the competitive economic landscape.

In regard to support spaces, personal lockers for shared workspaces, increased amenities, centralised filing and off-site storage are part of the considerations for a workplace.

Technology has enabled work to be mobile through the use of laptops and portable devices. And the internet has enabled all these devices to be connected. All a worker needs is a device to connect to the Internet, and he can virtually work at any place and at any time. Employees can now work remotely and no longer have to go to a specific location to work. The hours of work have also changed and there is no need to confine work to fixed office hours.

Negative effects of the changing workplace

The changes in the workplace and the resultant office layouts could lead to the following negative effects which need to be mitigated:

- Inefficiencies and risks, particularly increased noise, distractions and interruptions
- Challenges in communications
- Employee resistance to change
- Longer work hours

Table 9.3   Negative effects of changes in the workplace.

Change in the Workplace	Inefficiencies, Risks	Communications	Resistance	Longer Hours
1 Increased use of teams	Increased noise, distractions and interruptions.	Potential for "over communicating"	Resistance to change	Individuals working longer hours, expectation that workers are always available.
2 Greater use of dispersed work groups	High dependence on technology.	Loss of opportunity to develop trust through face to face interaction. More difficulty managing and coordinating.		Expansion of the workday to accommodate geographically dispersed team meetings.
3 Continual reorganisation and restructuring	Flexible layout might lead to increased noise and reduced ergonomic effectiveness.			
4 Reduce costs	Increased densities might lead to increased noise, distractions and interruptions. Smaller spaces are difficult for paper intensive work.		Increased densities might meet with employee resistance.	

(*Continued*)

Table 9.3   (*Continued*)

	Change in the Work-place	Inefficiencies, Risks	Communications	Resistance	Longer Hours
5	Improve quality of work life to attract and retain staff			Equitable spatial allocation might meet with resistance from those who support hierarchical space allocation.	

9.3 Essential #9 – Considerations in planning and design of offices

There are various reasons for an organisation to renovate the office or move to a new office: when the office becomes outdated or worn out, when the organisation expands or downsizes or in the case of rented premises, when the existing lease has ended or is renewed. This provides an opportunity for the organisation to create a new workspace that will meet the organisation's objectives.

The programming process introduced in Chapter 5 can be used in the context of an office. The process will be similar, though not as detailed, as the scale of the office is typically smaller than a whole building.

- Determine programming framework and identify project goals
- Evaluate existing conditions and facts
- Identify concepts and requirements
- Determine space requirements
- Produce programming report

Office project objectives

A key step in the office programming process is to determine the organisation's objectives for the new office. The following are some possible examples.

- Attract and retain talented employees
- Support a change in the organisational culture
- Promote creativity
- Project a good image of the company
- Promote teamwork
- Reduce cost
- Improve the satisfaction of employees
- Reduce environmental impact
- Increase collaboration

There needs to be a balance between the various combination of spaces: individual work spaces vs collaboration spaces, private spaces vs public spaces, concentration spaces vs discussion spaces.

An office can be divided into workspaces, meeting spaces and support spaces. We will now look at each area and the considerations for each of them.

Workspaces

The following concepts need to be considered:

- Working on site or remotely
- Individual assigned workspace or hot-desking
- Type of workspace
- Standardisation
- Physical file storage or electronic

The first concept that needs to be considered is whether employees are working on site or remotely. There is an increasing number of employees who are given the option to work remotely. These employees might only need to periodically return to the office, so they do not need a permanent assigned workspace. Allowing employees to work remotely could potentially reduce the number of workspaces required. However, there needs to be infrastructure (e.g. laptops, mobile devices, secure network connection) put in place to support a mobile workforce.

Provision of coworking space membership might be another way to support a mobile workforce.

The second concept that needs to be considered is whether employees will be assigned individual workspaces or whether these workspaces will be shared in a hot-desking format. Sharing of workspaces will reduce the number of the total number of workspaces required and reduce the amount of office space needed.

The third concept that needs to be considered is the type of workspace for each employee. The type of workspace for each employee could be an individual enclosed office or a desk in an open area. If the workspace has partitions, the height of the partitions has to be carefully considered as this will affect both visual privacy and the look and feel of the open office.

The fourth concept that needs to be considered is standardisation. Are all the desks going to be the same desks for all the departments in an organisation? For example, engineering departments might require bigger desks because of the need to handle drawings. However, the key benefit of standardisation is that it allows for easy reassignment of desks when there are organisational changes.

The fifth concept that needs to be considered is whether file storage is in a physical or electronic format. Physical file storage will require more space at the desk while electronic file storage will require Information Technology infrastructure.

In terms of area, a typical workstation is 6 to 9 square metres in size. A basic workstation will occupy about 6 square metres while an enclosed office is at least 9 square metres in size. For organisations that have employees that work on the go or remotely, hot desks need to be provided for them when they drop by at the office.

Meeting spaces

Meeting spaces can be meeting rooms or informal collaborative spaces. Meeting spaces require 1.5 to 2 square metres per person, with enclosed meeting spaces requiring more space than open meeting spaces.

The number and type of meeting spaces will depend on the organisation and type of meetings, which may vary from:

- Small or large meetings
- Project work
- Individual work vs collaborative work
- Private meetings

While there is still a need for meeting rooms for formal meetings, the rise of collaborative work has given rise to the need for more informal meeting spaces to support such type of work. For example, many organisations have transformed their pantries from rooms to open areas with island counters and seating areas resembling a café. These spaces serve as areas for staff to get coffee or other refreshments or use as an area for informal discussions or group work. Some organisations have even placed these areas adjacent to the office entrance using these spaces as visitor reception areas or meeting areas with their external vendors.

Support spaces

Various types of support spaces are required for offices. The following are examples of support spaces:

- printing area
- pantry
- reception area/ waiting area
- file rooms
- storage areas

The printing area should be placed in a separate area to reduce the noise and fumes. However, it should be relatively accessible for employees to collect their printouts. As offices become paperless, these facilities can be further consolidated and reduced.

Reception areas have generally become smaller. In some offices, the reception area, pantries and public meeting areas are all co-located for greater efficiency and allows for mixed-use and spill-over.

File rooms have generally become smaller with the advent of digital filing. Given the cost of space, many organisations have opted to use off site storage where records are boxed up and retrieved only when needed.

Storage areas have become smaller as most offices have gone electronic for many processes reducing the need for paper. In addition, just in time delivery of office supplies and equipment have also reduced the need for storage space for such items.

9.4 Challenges in implementing new office concepts

At the end of an office lease or when it is time for an office renovation, there is an opportunity to try out new office concepts. Sometimes, the implementation of a new office concept is part of a bigger reorganisation or transformation spearheaded by the organisation's executive team. It is also an opportunity for cultural change in the organisation when a change is needed from "business as usual".

What are some examples of major changes that can be made to an office? The following are some examples:

- Implement an open office concept where there are fewer or no private offices.
- Increase the amount of space for collaboration and reduce the individual office or desk space.
- Change from individual assigned desks to a hot-desking format where individuals are seated at whichever desks are available.
- To support a need for more meeting spaces, open meeting spaces could be built instead of enclosed meeting rooms.
- Reduction of the overall office footprint.

For major changes to an office layout especially those that could be perceived negatively, there needs to be support from the very top of the organisation. There must be buy in from the chief executive and the rest of the executive team.

There are three areas that need to be carefully considered in order to successfully implement a new office concept:

1. Clear communication with employees and keeping them engaged throughout the whole project
2. Involvement of the users in the process
3. Post-occupancy: receiving feedback and making improvements after move-in

Let us consider an example of an organisation whose offices are undergoing renovation. The old office was a mixture of private offices for the senior managers, full height partitions and cubicles for mid-level managers and half height partitions and cubicles for the remaining staff. The new office will be an 'open concept' office where all staff have a similar workstation. There are some half height partitions (on only one side) between desks for privacy but these do not enclose the entire workstation as in the old office.

The first area to focus on is communication. There is a need to keep employees engaged in the process. As part of the change management, there is a need to have town halls (large group meetings) and feedback sessions to address any major concerns that might arise. Explaining the rationale behind key decisions will help the majority support or not actively obstruct changes. For example, in an office that traditionally has assigned seating, where everyone has their individual workstations, the introduction of hot-desking (unassigned seating) in the office will require lots of communication as part of the change management process.

The second area to focus on is the involvement of the users so that they have a stake in the decisions and the new office space. Getting a few key users that have influence involved in the decision-making process will be helpful in getting buy in from the majority of the users.

One way to get them involved is to include them in the selection process for the colour of the partitions and the furniture in the new office. There can be a naming competition for the meeting rooms in the new office.

The third area to focus on is post-occupancy. After moving into the office, there will be a need to check on how the occupants are doing in their new spaces. There will be 'pain points' that need to be addressed. For example, the light sensors might not be programmed properly and turn off lights prematurely. There will be a need to establish new etiquette for the new office. There might be people hogging shared spaces by leaving their things there even when they are not in use. Signage would have to be put up to remind them that it is a shared space and not for one person's exclusive use. This process of post-occupancy monitoring will last for a few months before the occupants settle in and reach a steady state.

9.5 Coworking spaces

This section explores a growing trend in the workplace: Coworking spaces. Coworking spaces are shared office spaces used by a diverse group of people. Used initially by freelancers and entrepreneurs, they are growing in popularity and even becoming mainstream with large multinationals buying memberships for their staff to use these coworking spaces as a space for working.

The concept of 'serviced offices' has existed before the advent of coworking spaces. However, a key distinctive feature of coworking spaces that differentiates it from serviced offices is the "community" aspect of coworking spaces. Many coworking spaces have community managers to organise activities for their members to network and to relax. These community managers host events that might be of interest to their members. They are often membership-based, with users paying a monthly fee in exchange for the use of the shared office space.

With the growth in demand for coworking spaces, there are now coworking companies that operate multiple locations globally. WeWork is an example of such a company that has been expanding rapidly.

Starting from their first office in New York City, they now (as of August 2018) have 446 coworking locations in 86 cities, spread out over North America, Asia, Europe, South America, and Australia. Their customer base ranges from individuals to large companies.

What do the coworking spaces look like? The shared office space would include open desk areas or enclosed office spaces. There are also meeting spaces and other support spaces like pantries and printing areas. A coworking space looks like a traditional office space. The key difference is that it is built for sharing and there are spaces for people to build community and network.

Who uses these coworking spaces? The people using the coworking spaces range from freelancers to employees working remotely. They come from different industries and do different jobs. It also depends on the mode of operation for the coworking space in question. While some coworking spaces seek to attract a diverse customer base, some coworking spaces target people from a particular industry or a particular segment as part of their business model. For example, some coworking spaces have childcare available to attract working parents to their coworking space.

The reasons why people join coworking spaces vary. At the onset, coworking spaces were used by independent workers who did not have dedicated office spaces to work in. The first coworking spaces allowed these workers to have a space to work in other than their homes. Other reasons for coworking spaces include the following:

- It provides a community for users to plug into even though they do not have dedicated office spaces. They can interact with other people in the same industry or other industries in an office setting.
- It provides networking opportunities for its members. Often members can source for services from other members in a coworking community.
- Coworking is flexible. It removes the upfront costs of setting up an office as many coworking spaces charge a monthly fee and allow members the flexibility to terminate their membership at the end of

the month. The user need not be concerned with the operation of the office space. Meeting rooms, printing services and other amenities are also available for the members to use.

- Coworking spaces are located in convenient, accessible locations. Sometimes, there is the option of having more than one location to choose from. This makes it very useful for the mobile worker that travels from place to place or city to city in various countries.

Coworking spaces continue to evolve and are becoming more mainstream in terms of large corporations getting memberships for their employees. These large multinational companies do it for the following reasons:

- Some of their employees spend a lot of time going to various sites. Buying memberships for them with a coworking service provider with multiple locations globally will allow them to be productive even when they are travelling and away from the company's offices.
- It allows them to outsource the office function by replacing it with a service provider that specialises in providing office space that could help the employees work more productively.
- These coworking spaces have a diverse membership base. By placing employees in these spaces, they can build relationships and network with potential customers and buyers. Some coworking spaces have an 'entrepreneurial' vibe that a large company might want their employees to tap into and be affected by. By locating some of their employees in such spaces, it could help to influence and change their employee's mindset.

References

Gensler (2018), "Design Forecast", available at: https://www.gensler.com/research-insight/publications/design-forecast/2017 (accessed 12 Jun 2018)

Harvard Business Review (2015), "Why People Thrive in Coworking Spaces", available at: https://hbr.org/2015/05/why-people-thrive-in-coworking-spaces (accessed 12 Jun 2018)

Knight Frank (2016), "Guide to office leasing in Singapore", available at: http://www.knightfrank.com.sg/resources/pdfs/new-office-leasing-guide_16-june-2016.pdf (accessed 16 Aug 2018)

Myerson, J. (2013). Workplace Redesign to Support the 'Front End' of Innovation. In *Managing Organizational Ecologies* (pp. 41–51). Routledge.

WeWork (2018), "Locations", available at: https://www.wework.com/locations (accessed 23 Aug 18)

World Building Design Guide (2016), "The Changing Nature of Organisations, Work, and Workplace", available at: https://www.wbdg.org/resources/changing-nature-organizations-work-and-workplace (accessed 12 Jul 2018)

van Meel, J., Martens, Y., & van Ree, H. J. (2010). Planning office spaces: a practical guide for managers and designers. L. King.

CHAPTER 10

Space Management

In this chapter, you will learn about the following:

1. Importance of managing space in a facility
2. Gathering information about the space
3. Essential #10a – Creating or updating the space management policy
4. Essential #10b – Using technology for space management

Essential #10

Learn the principles of managing space in a large facility with a space management policy and software.

In a large facility, the facility manager is responsible for a large amount of space. This resource needs to be carefully managed. There are implications like cost of constructing and maintaining the space, productivity and well-being of the employees, and image of the organisation.

The facility manager needs to have an inventory of the spaces in his facility in order to manage them properly. He also needs to know how well they are used, what times they are used, and who are using them. He also needs to know the condition of the spaces and the type of furniture and equipment in each of the spaces.

There are many parties involved so there needs to be clear policies and processes to manage space so that this can be communicated to everyone involved.

If the spaces are worn down, they need to be repaired or renovated. If the spaces are inadequate, they need to be reconfigured or renovated or expanded.

Technology is often used to help keep track of the spaces in the facility.

10.1 Importance of managing space in a facility

In most organisations, the cost of space is typically the highest expenditure, second only to the salaries of employees. Space is an expensive resource — there is a high cost to construct the space and there is also the ongoing cost of occupying the space in terms of operating and maintaining the space.

For organisations that own property, the space can be rented out and serve as a source of income. The space occupied by a company can be used to create a corporate identity and brand. Good design and management of the space can improve the well-being of the occupants and increase productivity. Creative industries also fit out their working spaces to stimulate the creativity of occupants.

For state-funded universities (e.g. in the United States), the floor area needs to be reported for government grant purposes. Hence, it is important that all space used for education needs to be accurately reported so that the appropriate amount of grant funding is received. For some academic programmes (e.g. nursing programmes), the amount of space needs to be reported for the accreditation of the nursing school.

Challenges associated with space management

What are the problems faced by the facility manager regarding space management? The two key problems are having to manage a large portfolio of spaces and keeping track of the changes in this large portfolio.

A facility manager in a campus environment will typically have a large number of buildings. Each of the buildings are of varying sizes and will have different attributes as they are configured for different purposes at different times. Some buildings and spaces would have been repurposed from their original uses. As new buildings are constructed, this needs to be added to the portfolio.

The facility manager is also involved in move management. This involves arranging for moves and keeping track of where everyone is and which spaces are vacant and occupied.

For large portfolios, space management software is needed to track all the spaces in the portfolio. The software can be used to calculate space allocation and plan space moves. This will be expanded on in a later section of this chapter.

Implications of design on usability of space

The design of the space impacts the usability of the space which in turn impacts the management of the space. The space manager should have input in the design process for new buildings and spaces that are undergoing renovation in order to improve the usability of the spaces.

Let us now consider the implications of design in terms of architecture, structure, mechanical and electrical services.

In terms of architectural design, careful attention needs to be taken when designing the floor plate of the building. The shape of the floor plan impacts the amount of usable space. For example, a rectangular plan is easier to use than an octagonal floor plan. Another area that needs attention is the size of each workstation and the density of their distribution. The smaller the workstations in an area, the more workstations (i.e. staff) can be accommodated in the same footprint with only a slight increase in operational cost.

In terms of structural design, the type of the structure used will affect the usability of the space. The structural system, like the thickness of the beams, affect the floor to ceiling height. The location of columns will affect the usage of the room. For example, column-free spaces are needed for lecture rooms and large open offices. The permissible floor loadings will dictate what the room can be used for. In a university context, laboratories need to be designed with a higher floor loading (compared to staff offices) because of the weight of lab equipment.

In terms of mechanical and electrical services, does the space have sufficient services (e.g. air conditioning, electrical power, lighting, data) to be changed to other uses? Another area that will affect the usability of the space is the accessibility of the rooms via lifts and escalators. For example, rooms like auditoriums on upper floors will require escalators to facilitate the large flow of people entering or exiting the auditorium. Finally, for buildings with ducted air-conditioning systems, consideration needs to be given to the impact of large ducts in the ceiling which will impact the usable floor to ceiling height of the room.

10.2 Gathering information about the space

The Facility Manager is responsible for the use and management of space in an organisation's real estate portfolio. In order to do this, the facility manager needs to know the attributes of the various spaces under his care. These include the following:

- Dimensions of the space, the area of the space (in terms of square metres or hectares for larger spaces) and, in some cases, the height of the space and volume of the space.
- Occupants of the space (e.g. number of occupants) and the type of activities that take place in the space.
- Utilisation level of the space. For example, the percentage of time the space is occupied.

To give a sense of how large buildings are and the area of land they occupy, let us look at some examples. A typical primary school in Singapore has a floor area of about 20,000 square metres and sits on a site of just under 2 hectares (1 ha = 10,000 m²). The typical suburban shopping mall in Singapore has about 30,000 to 40,000 square metres of Net Lettable Area. On the higher end of the scale will be the Singapore Changi Airport Terminal 3 building with a floor area of

380,000 square metres and the entire airport (including two runways and four passenger terminals) occupies 1700 hectares of land.

Example: Gathering information about buildings on a university campus

Let us now consider the above-mentioned attributes of space in the context of a university campus. Many universities have large campuses with many buildings.

Dimensions of the space, the area of the space

First, the facility manager responsible for a campus should know what the area of the campus in terms of hectares, the number of buildings on campus and the total gross floor area of the buildings.

For example, the National University of Singapore's has three campuses in Singapore housing 17 schools, 35,000 students and 12,000 faculty and staff. The main campus at Kent Ridge is 150 hectares in size.

All the floor plans of the buildings, especially the key buildings, should be available as a reference. This can be placed on the university's intranet for easy access. However, floor plans for buildings with restricted access should not be placed on the intranet for security reasons.

Occupants of the space and the type of activities that take place in the space

A list of the rooms in each building should be made with the corresponding floor area for each room. There are diverse room types within each building and between buildings across campus. There are teaching spaces (e.g. lecture theatres, tutorial rooms), research spaces (e.g. laboratories), libraries, offices and recreational spaces. Some of these spaces are for the exclusive use of one person or group while others are shared.

At a university, the space database should have information on which university unit or department is responsible for the various rooms in each building for accountability purposes.

Utilisation level of the space

In order to manage space effectively, information on the utilisation level of the space needs to be collected. At a university, the usage patterns of the lecture theatres and the tutorial rooms can be obtained from the university timetabling system. For offices, this could be obtained during the annual space audit when the usage levels are collected.

Additional information that can be collected for Facility Management purposes

With the baseline information collected, this database can be made available to other departments in the University. These other departments can collect additional information to overlay onto the space database.

For example, additional information can be collected to be put on the internet to help visitors and new staff and students to find their way around the university campus. Information for wayfinding purposes include:

- Picture of the building
- Opening hours of each building (hours accessible)
- Address and geographical coordinates
- Parking and public transport

The Facilities Maintenance and Services Department could provide information about facilities maintenance and services to the users of the buildings on the internet or university intranet. Information provided could include:

- Name and contact information of the Building Supervisor: This allows the users to contact the supervisor directly for any non-routine request or inquiry.
- Maintenance of the space: Users can request maintenance or find out the status of maintenance requests and projects.
- Cleaning service and waste disposal: availability and timing.

- Cost of operating the building: This could include the amount and cost of utilities like electricity and water. This could motivate users to help in sustainability efforts to reduce the use of energy and water.
- Health and Safety maps: this could be used for evacuation purposes during emergencies.

10.3   Essential #10a – Creating or updating the space management policy

Because of the large number of users in a facility, there is a need for guidelines on the use of space. This usually takes the form of a space management policy.

The space management policy will contain the following:

- The authority for allocation of space
- Responsibilities of the various parties involved in managing space (e.g. Space Planner, Space Committee, Heads of Departments)
- Process for allocation of space (for both existing space and new space)
- Process for reporting changes in use of space
- Conducting space audits

Universities need to have a space management policy. Many universities are public entities that require careful stewardship of the assets which includes buildings. There are many competing uses for facilities among the large and diverse number of users.

Many universities have ownership of their campus and the buildings. The university is built out in phases over many years. New buildings and spaces are built to keep up with new needs. There is a need to renovate spaces that are aging to renew them and bring them up to statutory requirements and new standards. There is also a need to repurpose spaces whose existing use is no longer needed.

Authority for allocation of space

The ultimate authority for allocation of space resides with the Chief Executive of the organisation. This ensures that the use of space supports the organisation's key objectives. The physical space may be owned or leased by the organisation. The space could be assigned to a department to use. The control of the use of the space may be delegated by the Chief Executive of the organisation to the Heads of Department.

In terms of space management policy, this is delegated to the Head of Facilities and Space Committee (made up of representatives from different parts of the organisation) to evaluate space requests and ensure that the space in the organisation is used to advance the most important priorities of the organisation.

In a university, the final authority for the allocation of space is the President of the University and the control of the use of the space may be delegated to the Deans of the various faculties of the University so that each faculty can respond quickly to their own needs.

Responsibilities of the various parties involved in managing space

There are various parties involved in managing the space in an organisation. Their responsibilities in space management are outlined in the table below.

Table 10.1   Parties involved in managing space in an organisation.

	Title	Responsibilities
1	Chief Executive	• Final authority for allocation of space
2	Head of Facilities	• Identify priorities for space in alignment with organisation's Strategic Plan
		• Ensure that new space and facilities are consistent with organisation's facilities master plan
		• Improve usage of space
		• Improve efficiency of space use

	Title	Responsibilities
3	Space Committee	• Assist the Head of Facilities
4	Space Planner	• Reports to the Head of Facilities • Conduct space survey • Ensure accuracy of space database • Generate space inventories

Process for allocation of space

There are various ways for the allocation of space. The space in an organisation can be managed in a centralised or decentralised manner. The control of space was previously decentralised because of the inability to keep track of large amounts of space centrally. With the advent of information technology, space can be administered in a cost-effective manner. New space is created through construction projects. The decision to create new space and the allocation of this new space is based on the priorities of the organisation.

Where possible, the sharing of facilities should be done to reduce the amount of space needed. This also has the potential to defer or reduce capital investment in new buildings. For example, lecture rooms and classrooms that can be shared among the whole university could help to increase utilisation and reduce the need for additional rooms.

Process for reporting changes in use of space

Over the years, there will be changes to the use of the various spaces. There needs to be a process in place for reporting changes to the use of space. Every room needs to be identified with a unique alphanumeric code. This is needed for maintenance fault reporting, etc. Like all databases, it needs to be maintained for accuracy. This database will be useful for other facility software programs like room scheduling software.

An example of room information that would be captured in a space database are listed below:

• Building
• Room

- Room Type
- Department
- Description
- Usage
- Room dimensions and area

Conducting space audits

To ensure the accuracy of the space database, it is good practice to conduct a space audit annually and produce an annual report detailing the amount of space, how the space is used and utilisation levels. This provides feedback to management for improved decision making. It is also an opportunity to update the space database to keep it up to date. It can be used to decide and justify the need for new space or more space.

For example, in some organisations, a mandatory audit is required every five years. Audits should be conducted annually to reconcile the inventory. Buildings that were recently renovated need to be audited for possible change of use of areas. For organisations with a large campus, a few buildings can be audited each month. Ranking criteria for which buildings to check first should be set up with the larger and more important buildings being done first, followed by smaller and less critical buildings.

Space audits should be conducted once a year for offices. Ideally, this should be conducted when most people are around so that the utilisation rate will not be underreported. For consistency, it should be done at the same time every year.

Methods of data collection include observations, surveys of users, interviews and sampling.

10.4 Essential #10b – Using technology for space management

In order to manage space in a large facility, it is critical to harness technology and use space management software. Examples of such software include Archibus and Planon.

In many companies, much of the space management process is still manual and paper-based. There is basic use of technology like spreadsheet software; however, the information cannot be viewed by other staff and there is limited sharing of the information.

Often, the space managers and staff work with paper floor plans. Changes are marked and hand-drawn on the floor plans. These changes are then updated by the CAD staff on the electronic floor plans. A new copy is then printed out for staff to refer to. Similarly, room inventories are manually updated on spreadsheet software and not connected or integrated with other enterprise software solutions.

Benefits of space management software

The biggest benefit of using space management software is that it can act as a single source of space information and drawings, reducing the confusion and inaccuracy of multiple sources. When properly populated and managed, it will be recognised as the official source of space information for the organisation. Other parts of the organisation can be given access to this database so that it can be leveraged to improve performance.

Space management software are able to manage large areas and a large number of floor plans in multiple buildings over many locations globally. It allows for the analysis of space information to identify critical issues. This helps the organisation to optimise space use and utilise space strategically to further the corporate objectives. The space information provides management with data to make decisions. Trends can be identified, 'what if' scenarios can be run to test various ideas and space can be aligned with the strategic goals of the company.

The space management software will be able to improve the efficiency and productivity of the organisation. By keeping track of vacant workstations, the software can assist in the speedy onboarding of new employees. It can also run various scenarios as part of move management when there is a need to shift employees around as a result of organisational changes.

The space management software when integrated with other systems (e.g. security system, tenant management system, work order management system) will be able to automatically update the space information in these systems, improving efficiency and productivity. The software coupled with mobile technology allows staff issued with tablets to access the space database on the go instead of having to return to their desks to check the database.

Challenges with space management software

There are some challenges with using space management software that need to be considered. An adequate amount of manpower and resources need to be committed to maintaining the space management database. It takes a lot of effort and time to populate the space database. The data needs to be collected or transferred from older software programmes or old hardcopy records and verified and checked for accuracy and completeness. It takes a lot of resources to maintain the space database as changes to space information because of new construction, renovations or moves need to be captured.

The space management software might not be fully compatible with other enterprise systems. This would mean that there might only be partial integration and workarounds will need to be worked out to achieve the functionality of automatic updating that is desired.

Security levels and settings need to be carefully considered to prevent sharing of confidential space information with unauthorised personnel.

Because of the specialised nature of space management software, there would be a limited pool of people that can manage the software effectively. These staff members will need to be sent for regular training to keep them up to date in order to realise the full potential of the system. There are also a large number of department space representatives that also need training to learn how to use the software so that they can input updates into the system for their respective departments.

Functions of space management software

In terms of space management, the software should have the following functions:

- Inventory: database of buildings, floor plans, areas, rooms, etc.
- Space allocation: the ability to allocate spaces to different work groups and people
- Chargeback function: the ability to monitor how much area each department uses and create an internal charging mechanism where each department 'pays' for the area used.
- Move management: to plan moves for groups of staff and create various scenarios before executing the actual move

Ideally the software used should be integrated with other aspects of facility management like building operations, workplace services, asset management and capital project management.

The software should be able to present information in a clear fashion. It should have a dashboard with the following information:

- Number of buildings
- Gross area
- Operating cost
- Occupancy
- Lease information
- Type of use
- Breakdown by geographical area (for large portfolios)

Archibus is an example of space management software popular with many universities. The inventory function allows universities to easily track usage and generate reports for state-funded universities that are accountable to the public. There is a standardised way of naming buildings, facilities and rooms on campus. In addition to a 'space management' committee', there needs to be representatives at each university unit that are trained to update the database as necessary.

References

Archibus (2018), "Space Planning Management", available at: https://archibus.com/products/space-planning-management/ (accessed 22 Jul 2018)

National University of Singapore (2017), "NUS Annual Report", available at: http://www.nus.edu.sg/annualreport/pdf/nus-annualreport-2017.pdf (accessed 27 Aug 2018)

National University of Singapore (2018), "Welcome to NUS", available at: http://www.nus.edu.sg/images/resources/content/about/welcome-to-nus.pdf (accessed 27 Aug 2018)

Planon (2018), "Space and Workplace Management", available at: https://planonsoftware.com/us/solutions/space-workplace-management-software/ (accessed 22 Jul 2018)

Sam Houston State University (2018), "Facilities Space Management", available at: https://www.shsu.edu/facilities-space-management/ (accessed 12 Jul 2018)

Teicholz, E. (2013). *Technology for facility managers*. Hobokn, New Jersey: John Wiley.

Wiggins, J. M. (2010). *Facilities manager's desk reference*. John Wiley & Sons.

Index

accessibility, 61, 84
    code, 63
activity grouping, 84
adults, 59
    dimensions, 57
air emissions, 119
air pollutants, 119
airport, 107, 130, 143
    capital improvement projects, 143
    environmental impact assessment, 130
    facility master plan, 107
    space standards, 67
    strategic plan, 31
air quality, 119
alternative concepts for master plans, 106
American Planning Association, 98
anthropometrics, 56
architect, 16, 43
    role, 43
architectural design, 175
architectural Programming, 72
area, 165
    gross floor area, 65
    net floor area, 65
area definitions, 64
authority for space allocation, 180

benefits of space management software, 183
benefits of strategic planning, 23
biodiversity, 120
Building and Construction Authority, 63, 103
building efficiency factors, 66
build phase, 13

campus master plan, 33
campus planning and design, 18
capital budget, 138, 149
capital costs, 138
capital improvement plan, 9, 140
    process, 140
    report, 149
capital improvement planning, 137, 138, 140
    cost estimate, 146
    funding sources, 146
    importance, 140
    management, 139
    prioritisation criteria, 147
    process, 140
    project information, 144
    project justification, 145
    project list, 142, 148
    project requests, 143
    project schedule, 146
    steps, 141

capital improvement plan report, 149
capital improvement projects, 138
    Examples, 143
capital planning managers, 139
challenges associated with space
    management, 174
challenges with space management
    software, 184
change in the workplace, 158
changing workplace, 162
character, 82
civil and structural engineer, 16, 43
    role, 43
code on accessibility, 63
communications, 84
community in coworking spaces,
    169
components of a facility master
    plan, 101
comprehensive plan, 98
concepts in workspaces, 164
construction, 13, 87
construction phase, 13
consultant, 7, 11, 16, 42
    evaluation criteria, 49
    evaluation criteria - weightage,
        51
    selection process, 7, 47
contents of a strategic brief, 44
contractor, 16
corridor
    widths, 59
    widths - wheelchair, 61
corridor widths, 59, 61
cost control, 87
cost estimate, 146
costs, 101
coworking, 169
coworking spaces, 169
    community, 169
    design, 170

memberships, 171
    users, 170
coworking spaces layout, 170
cultural resources, 121
civil and structural engineer, 16
    role, 43

decision, 128
definitions for EIA, 124
density, 83
design, 4
    architectural, 175
    consultants, 47
    corridor, 59
    importance, 4
    mechanical and electrical, 176
    office, 158, 163
    Owner's role, 37
    stages, 12
    structural, 175
    workplace, 10, 157
design of an office, 158
design of corridors, 59
design phase, 12
development, 38
    parties involved, 7, 15
    phases, 7, 14, 38
development of a building, 7
development plan, 106
dimensions, 60
    corridor widths, 59
    moving adults, 59
    sitting adults, 58
    standing adults, 57
    wheelchairs, 60
dimensions of sitting adults, 58
dimensions of standing adults, 57

EIA legislation in Singapore, 126
EIA process, 127
elderly, 63

electrical engineer, 16
energy conservation, 87
environmental, 87
environmental control, 87
environmental impact, 9, 118
    examples, 123
environmental impact assessment
    (EIA), 9
    decision, 128
    definition, 124
    legislation, 124
    legislation - European Union,
        125
    legislation - Hong Kong, 125
    legislation - Singapore, 126
    legislation - United States, 125
    mitigation measures, 128
    process, 124, 127
    public consultation, 128
    scoping, 128
    screening, 127
    stakeholders, 129
environmental issue, 123
environmental laws
    Singapore, 123
    United States, 123
environmental legislation, 122
environmental permit, 129
environmental planning, 9, 117
essentials of facilities planning and
    design
    definition, 3
    essentials, 3
establishing space requirements, 45
European Union, 125
evaluation criteria
    consultants, 49
evaluation criteria for consultant, 49
examples, 104
    capital improvement projects,
        143

environmental impacts, 123
    facility master plans, 103
execution and monitoring of the
    strategic plan, 26
existing conditions, 77

facilities planning and design, 18
    definition, 3
    essentials, 3, 18
    importance, 4
facility life
    build phase, 13
    construction phase, 13
    design phase, 12
    management phase, 13
    phases, 10
    planning phase, 10
facility management, 5
facility manager, 6, 17, 21, 27,
    139, 173
    strategic planning, 21, 27
facility master plan, 7, 9, 21, 33, 100,
    142
    airport, 107
    costs, 101
    examples, 103, 104
    phasing, 101
    program requirements, 101
    regulatory requirements, 101
    stakeholders, 102
    university, 110
facility master planning, 21, 97
    alternative concepts, 106
    development plan, 106
    examples, 103
    facility requirements, 105
    forecasts, 105
    implementation plan, 106
    inventory, 104
    process, 104
facility requirements, 105

file storage, 165
flexibility, 85
forecasts, 105
functional brief, 72
functions of space management
    software, 185
funding sources, 146

globalisation, 158
greenhouse gas, 119
gross floor area, 65

hierarchy, 82
historic, 121
historic resources, 121
Hong Kong, 125
hospital, 152
    capital improvement project,
    152
hot-desking, 164

implementation plan, 106
implementing new office concepts,
    167
importance of facilities planning
    and design, 4
importance of managing space,
    174
importance of space management,
    10
importance of the capital
    improvement planning process,
    140
information, 144
information about the space, 176
Information and Communications
    Technology (ICT), 158
information gathering techniques,
    74
inventory, 104

justification for project, 145

land contamination, 120
life of a facility, 10
list of potential projects, 142
list of projects, 148

maintenance, 13
manage phase, 13
master planning, 9, 104
    process, 9
measurement methods, 64
mechanical and electrical engineer,
    16, 43
    role, 43
mechanical and electrical services,
    176
meeting spaces, 160, 165
    type, 166
membership in coworking spaces,
    171
mission, 22
mitigation measures, 128
mixed flow, 86
moving, 59

need for programming, 73
neighbourhood plan, 98
neighbours, 83
net floor area, 65
noise pollution, 122

office
    design, 158
    meeting spaces, 160
    objectives, 163
    planning and design, 163
    post-occupancy, 169
    programming, 163
    support spaces, 160, 166

technology, 160
workspaces, 160
office concepts
   implementation, 167
office project objectives, 163
organisation, 41
orientation, 85
owner organisation, 15
Owner
   planning and design, 37
Owner's Representative, 6, 7, 11,
   37
   responsibilities, 7, 38, 39, 40
Owner's role, 37

parties, 7
parties involved in managing
   space, 180
parties involved in the
   development of a building, 15
people
   disabilities, 60
   wheelchairs, 60
people grouping, 83
people with disabilities, 60
phases, 7, 10, 38
phases of a development, 14
phasing, 87, 101
planners, 25
   roles, 25
planning, 4
   importance, 4
planning, and design, 37
   campus, 18
   essentials, 4
   offices, 163
   Owner's role, 37
   workplace, 10, 18, 157
planning and design of offices, 163
planning and design of workplaces,
   10

planning phase, 11
post-occupancy, 169
preparation of the strategic plan,
   26
principles of Universal Design, 61
prioritisation criteria, 147
priority, 82
process for allocation of space,
   181
process for programming, 76
process for reporting changes,
   181
programmatic concepts, 78, 80, 81
   accessibility, 84
   activity grouping, 84
   categories, 81
   character, 82
   communications, 84
   cost control, 87
   density, 83
   energy conservation, 87
   environmental control, 87
   flexibility, 85
   hierarchy, 82
   mixed flow, 86
   neighbours, 83
   orientation, 85
   people grouping, 83
   phasing, 87
   priority, 82
   relationships, 83
   safety, 86
   security, 86
   separated flow, 86
   sequential flow, 86
   service grouping, 84
   tolerance, 85
programmer, 74
programming, 8, 12, 71, 163
   buildings, 72
   existing conditions, 77

framework, 77
information gathering, 74
levels, 74
levels of programming, 74
need for, 72
offices, 163
process, 76
programmatic concepts, 78
programmer, 74
project goals, 77
report, 79
room data sheets, 79, 80
space requirements, 79
programming framework, 77
programming of buildings, 72
programming report, 79
program requirements, 101
project, 144
project goals, 77
project management, 41
    organisation, 41
project manager, 16, 37
project requests, 143
project schedule, 146
public consultation, 128

quantity surveyor, 16, 43
    role, 43

ramp gradients, 61
regulatory agencies, 17
regulatory requirements, 78, 101
relationships, 83
requirements
    regulatory, 78
    space, 79
    sustainability, 79
    user, 78
responsibilities, 7, 39, 40
responsibilities of the OwnerRep, 38
roles of planners, 25
room data sheet, 79, 80

safety, 86
scoping, 128
screening, 127
security, 86
selecting design consultants, 7
selection process for design
    consultants, 47
separated flow, 86
service grouping, 84
shortcomings, 23
Singapore
    Concept Plan, 99
    Government Budget, 149
    Master Plan, 99
Singapore Concept Plan, 99
Singapore environmental laws, 123
Singapore Government Budget, 149
Singapore Master Plan, 99
site evaluation criteria, 89, 90
site evaluation form, 91
site selection, 8, 71
    evaluation criteria, 88
    process, 88
site selection process, 88
socioeconomic impacts, 122
space
    accessibility, 61
    usability, 175
    human requirements, 56
space and humans, 56
space audits, 182
space management, 10, 173
    challenges, 174
    importance, 174
    information, 176
    policy, 10
    software, 10, 175
    technology, 182
space management policy, 10, 179
    authority, 180
    parties involved, 180
    reporting changes, 181

space allocation process, 181
space management software, 10,
   175, 182
   benefits, 183
   challenges, 184
   functions, 185
space requirements, 45, 79
spaces accessible, 61
space standards, 8, 55, 66
stakeholders, 129
   Government, 102
   in the strategic planning
      process, 27
steps in the capital improvement
   planning process, 141
steps in the master planning
   process, 104
strategic brief, 38, 43, 71, 72
   contents, 44
strategic goals, 22
strategic plan, 7, 22, 23, 142
   drives facility needs, 27
   execution, 26
   monitoring, 26
   preparation, 26
strategic plan drives the need for
   facilities, 27
strategic planning, 21, 22, 23
   benefits, 23
   process, 25
   shortcomings, 23
   stakeholders, 27
strategic planning process, 25
structural design, 175
structural engineer, 16
support spaces, 160, 166
sustainability requirements, 79
SWOT analysis, 26

technology, 160
technology for space management,
   182

ten essentials of facilities planning
   and design, 18
tolerance, 85
town planning, 98
transportation plan, 98
type of meeting spaces, 166
type of workspace, 165
types of urban plans, 98

United States, 125
Universal Design, 8, 55, 61, 64
   principles, 61
university, 34, 110, 177
   facility master plan, 110
   space management, 177
   strategic plan, 34
urban plan, 98
   comprehensive plan, 98
   neighbourhood plan, 98
   transportation plan, 98
urban planning, 82, 98
Urban Redevelopment Authority,
   64, 65, 98, 99, 103
usability of space, 175
user requirements, 78
   user, 78
US federal environmental laws, 123
utilisation level, 176

vision, 22
visually impaired, 63

waste management, 121
water quality, 119
weightage, 51
what is a facility master plan, 100
wheelchairs, 60–63
   corridor widths, 61
   dimensions, 60
   ramp gradients, 61
who uses these coworking spaces,
   170

workplace, 158
    changing, 158, 162
    planning and design, 10, 157
workplace planning and design, 18, 157

workspace, 160, 164
    area, 165
    file storage, 165
    type, 165

Titles of Interest

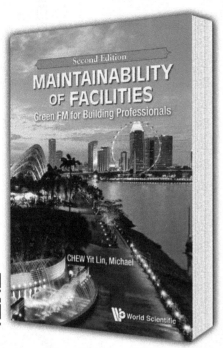

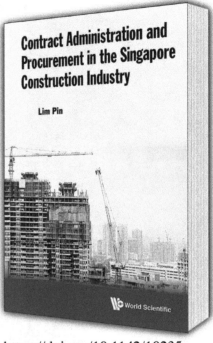

https://doi.org/10.1142/9832 https://doi.org/10.1142/10235

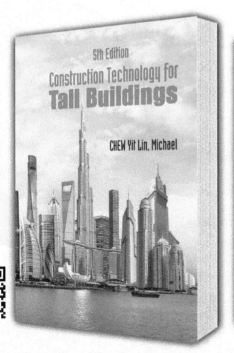

https://doi.org/10.1142/10465 https://doi.org/10.1142/10722

Titles of Interes

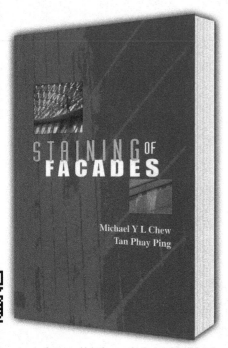

STAINING OF
FACADES

Michael Y L Chew
Tan Phay Ping

Nature,
Place &
People

Forging Connections through
Neighbourhood Landscape Design

Edited by
Tan Puay Yok, Liao Kuei-Hsien, Hwang Yun Hye & Vincent Chua

https://doi.org/10.1142/5216   https://doi.org/10.1142/10879

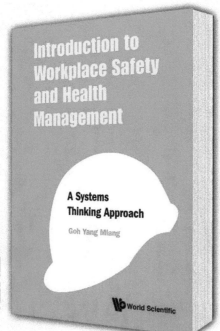

Introduction to
Workplace Safety
and Health
Management

A Systems
Thinking Approach

Goh Yang Miang

World Scientific

https://doi.org/10.1142/11094